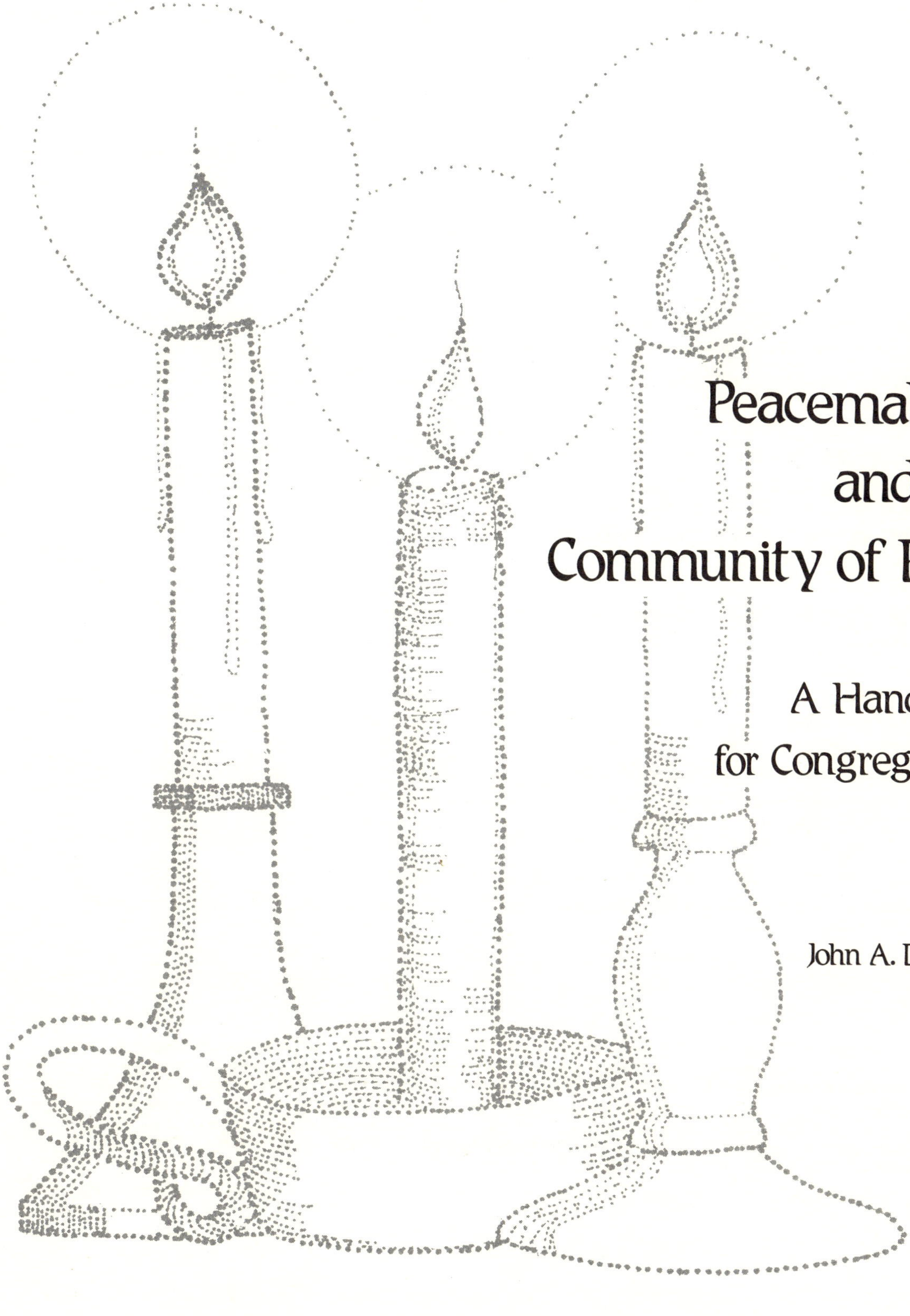

Peacemaking and the Community of Faith

A Handbook for Congregations

John A. Donaghy

Acknowledgements

ISBN: 0-8091-5181-2

Published by Paulist Press, 545 Island Road, Ramsey, N.J. 07446

Printed and bound in the United States of America

Written by John A. Donaghy

John A. Donaghy is a doctoral candidate in philosophy and a teaching fellow at Boston College. In 1980, he was Peace Coordinator for the Vermont Ecumenical Council. In 1979, he helped organize the local chapter of the Fellowship of Reconciliation (FOR) in Scranton, Pa. He is currently a member of the FOR National Council.

Project coordinated by Dan R. Ebener (Director of Covenant Peacemaking Program, FOR)

For their assistance and comments on this project:
Ann Albam (Director of Printing Production, FOR)
Richard Chartier (Editor, *Fellowship*)
Richard Baggett Deats (Executive Secretary, FOR)
Michael Jendrzejczyk (Director of Disarmament, FOR)
Diane Leonetti (Associate Editor, *Fellowship*)
Shirley Maynard (Staff, Covenant Peacemaking Program)
Rabbi Michael Robinson (Temple Israel, Croton-on-Hudson, N.Y.)
Sue and Chuck Ruehle (Directors, Lutheran Human Relations Association)

For sharing published and unpublished materials:
Mary Skinner (Peacemaking Project of the United Presbyterian Church in the U.S.A.)
Arthur Waskow (Public Resource Center)

For providing the author with the opportunity to work in the religious community of Vermont in 1980: Vermont Ecumenical Council Peace Committee

Special thanks to the Car-Eth Foundation for providing a grant for this project.

Design by: Vittoria Lenzi

CREDITS: Title page, Covenant Peacemaking Program, FOR; p. 1, Graphic by FOR/AFSC Nuclear Weapons Facilities Project; p. 2. *Friends Journal;* pp. 3, 4, 5, 6, *Fellowship,* p. 7. Peace Sabbath 1981; p. 9, Prayer for Peace (London); p. 10, Thompson Coventry Photo; p. 15, United Presbyterian Peace Fellowship; p. 19, Another Mother for Peace; p. 20, Pax Christi; p. 23, Photo by John Donaghy; p. 25, War Resisters' League; p. 27, *Reconciliation Quarterly* (London); p. 28, Covenant Peacemaking Program, FOR; p. 29, Photo by John Donaghy; p. 31, Photo by Jack Payden-Travers; p. 33, FOR/AFSC Nuclear Weapons Facilities Project; p. 35, Photo by Miriam Leader; pp. 36, 40, Sojourners; page 44: Copyright 1981 The Oklahoma Publishing Company, From *The Daily Oklahoman,* Aug. 10, Photo by David Longstreath.

First printing, 1/82; second printing (revised edition), 9/82

Fellowship Publications

Table of Contents

Introduction. The Critical Juncture — **1**

1. Peacemaking: An Integral Dimension of the Life of Faith — **4**

2. Peacemaking, Prayer, and Worship — **7**

Prayer and the Peacemaker
Corporate Worship and Peace — 8
Suggestions for Incorporating Peace in Worship — 9
Peace in Worship Services — 9
Peace Services — 11
Resources

3. Educating for Peace in the Congregation — **15**

Beginning Educational Efforts — 16
Congregational Study Groups — 18
Integrating Peace into Congregational Programs — 19
Education Programs for Youth — 20
Adult Education — 21
Ongoing Peace Education — 21
Interfaith Peace Efforts — 22
Interfaith Convocations — 22
Other Possible Efforts — 23
Resources

4. Activities for Peace — **25**

Congregational Activities — 26
The Congregation As Witness — 27
Congregational Public Witness — 28
Witness from Denominational Bodies — 30
Witness of Individuals — 31
Resources

5. The Nuclear Weapon Freeze Campaign — **33**

6. The New Abolitionist Covenant — **36**

Texts of the New Abolitionist Covenant — 37

Selected Resources — **41**

Books — 41
Periodicals — 41
Audiovisual Resources — 41
FOR Brochures — 42
Organizations — 42

Introduction. The Critical Juncture

Billy Graham at Auschwitz, 1978

The world is at a critical point, a time full of danger but also one of opportunity.

The greatest danger of our time is the international arms race. The arsenals of the world are growing at an alarming rate, increasing tensions throughout the world and fueling, at this moment, over 30 armed conflicts. The price of this arms race — over 550 billion dollars a year — guts the economies of almost all the nations of the world and inflicts massive burdens on the poor peoples of this earth.

A special danger is posed by the nuclear arms race. The nuclear powers have manufactured over 50,000 nuclear weapons; these stockpiles of mass destruction are growing in both numbers and sophistication. Despite over 6000 meetings to discuss nuclear arms limitation, the nations of the world have not dismantled a single nuclear weapon. In fact, the USA alone plans to manufacture 17,000 new nuclear weapons in the next decade.

The reasons given for the arms race are many. But we must ask, "To what end?" These weapons waste money. They utilize valuable human and natural resources. They divert scarce funds from meeting vital human needs.

And they do not make the world secure.

Rather, it seems that the more weapons there are and the more money spent on instruments of destruction, the more dangerous the world becomes.

It is essential that we read the signs of the times and face the crisis that has come upon us.

"The whole world has come under threat . . . From now on, it is only through a conscious choice and through a deliberate policy that humanity can survive."

Pope John Paul II at Hiroshima, 1981

In the face of this unprecedented threat to human survival, many people are seeking to find a way out and to move the nations of the world toward disarmament. The past few years have seen the burgeoning of groups world-wide in opposition to the arms race and in particular against nuclear weapons.

Europe has seen the inauguration of E.N.D., European Nuclear Disarmament, a campaign to make Europe a nuclear free zone from Portugal to Poland. In Great Britain, the Campaign for Nuclear Disarmament has re-emerged as a major force in political and civil life. In the Netherlands and Germany, there have been outcries against the neutron bomb and the scheduled placement of U.S. long-range nuclear missiles within their borders.

The United States has also experienced a growing concern for peace. Local groups are sprouting up all over the nation. There are now local Fellowship of Reconciliation (FOR) chapters from Cape Cod to San Diego. Many peace organizations have experienced revivals, especially the Physicians for Social Responsibility. Minority, labor, and feminist groups have been stressing the sufferings inflicted on the poor, on workers, and on women as spending for arms increases at the expense of human needs and at the cost of inflation. And a campaign for bilateral nuclear weapons freeze is receiving enthusiastic support from all sectors of American life and politics, especially at the grassroots level. Petition drives in many states and referenda in local communities in Massachusetts, Vermont, and New Hampshire indicate a growing desire for such an alternative.

The psychic numbing which has affected so many, the amnesia about the horrors of nuclear war, the moral apathy in the face of preparations for mass destruction — all these defenses against the bomb are slowly crumbling.

The horrors and the evils of nuclear weaponry are coming to the forefront of the consciousness of the people of the world.

The time of danger can become the time of opportunity.

"Today, as we know, the spirit has less authority than ever, but there are world hours in which, despite all obstacles, the authority of the spirit suffices to undertake the rescue of man [sic]. Such an hour appears to me to draw near.

Martin Buber, 1952

There are signs of a growing concern within the religious communities of the world. As a 1980 resolution of

Chinese character: "Crisis, danger, and opportunity."

the Church of the Brethren put it, "Times of crisis in the life of the religious community often create landmarks along the pilgrimage of faith."

International religious bodies have begun to address the arms race in ever more forceful terms. In November 1981, the World Council of Churches is sponsoring an international hearing on nuclear weapons and disarmament.

National, denominational, and ecumenical bodies have also put the issue on their agenda. The Interchurch Council in the Netherlands has been a major force in moving the Netherlands Reformed Church to call for the removal of all nuclear weapons from that country. Church leaders from the USA and the USSR have met twice to consider their common concerns for promoting disarmament. The National Council of Churches held a major consultation on disarmament in 1980. Project Ploughshares, supported by the Canadian Council of Churches, is eliciting support in Canada for alternative Canadian defense policies, especially in regard to NATO and the presence of nuclear weapons on Canadian soil.

In the United States, many religious bodies, ranging from the New Call to Peacemaking conferences of the historic peace churches and the General Synod of the United Church of Christ to the Southern Baptist Convention and the First Presidency of the Church of Jesus Christ of the Latter-Day Saints (Mormons) , have written major statements in opposition to the growing nuclear arms race. The United Methodist Church and the United Presbyterian Church have made significant commitments nationally to peacemaking. Many prominent American religious leaders have begun to speak forcefully against preparations for mass destruction. These have included not only people from "mainline" religious groups, such as Rev. William Sloane Coffin, Bishop Thomas Gumbleton, and Rabbi Balfour Brickner; but, more recently, evangelicals and many others have been questioning the arms race in light of their faith.

The Riverside Church Disarmament Program in New York and the Interfaith Center to Reverse the Arms Race in Los Angeles have initiated interfaith convocations and programs which have been copied in more than 200 communities throughout the nation.

Several denominations have recently hired new staff to work specifically with peace concerns. Some local churches and councils of churches have directed their staff to make reversing the arms race a priority. And several state ecumenical councils have hired staff to bring the message of peace and disarmament to local congregations.

Many people of faith are becoming advocates of peace. But many more continue to support policies that threaten the lives of millions. Many continue to work in factories and laboratories that manufacture or design components for nuclear weapons and weapons systems. And there are many people in positions of power who openly profess their faith while they continue to press for increases in military spending and for more nuclear weaponry.
Why?

> *"What the world expects of Christians is that Christians should speak out, loud and clear, and that they should voice their condemnation in such a way that never a doubt, never the slightest doubt, could rise in the heart of the simplest person. That they should get away from abstraction and confront the blood-stained face history has taken on today."*
> Albert Camus, 1948
>
> Camus, 1948

Though many denominations and religious leaders have spoken out against the bomb, there is still that residue of support for a massive arms build-up among many people who are members of the religious communities. Some of these people may have never heard these messages of peace. Or perhaps they have never taken time to carefully consider them. Others may have heard them but a distrust of statements from national and international bodies has prevented them from going beyond a purely political consideration of the issues. For some, their faith may have become entangled with an unthinking and uncritical patriotism. For many, an unexamined fear of the Soviets has led them to look for security in weapons of mass destruction. For most, however, it appears that national security has become identified with massive armaments, with being "number one," and with reliance on force alone to decide conflicts. An alternative vision of security, perhaps best expressed by the biblical concept of *shalom*, may have never crossed their minds. For these, or for other reasons, many deeply religious persons are suspicious of calls for disarmament or even adamantly opposed to them.

It is therefore important that concerned people seek to find ways to speak to the majority of people in the synagogues, temples, churches, and meeting houses throughout the United States, challenging them to deal with the issues of war and peace, the threat of nuclear war, and the moral dilemmas posed by U.S. military policies. People need to see that these are not merely political issues. They are, at base, moral and spiritual issues. They are problems which challenge the integrity of the religious communities of this and other nations and represent not just a crisis for the world but a crisis of faith.

"We must remind ourselves that both God and history will judge us severely if we fail to bring this matter to the attention of all the nations of the earth. I know the issues are complex and long-standing distrust and suspicion are not easily overcome. However, this must not keep us from our responsibility."

Billy Graham in a letter on the
arms race to Bishop Karoly Toth
of Hungary, 1979

This handbook is conceived as a guide to those who seek to bring their concern for peace and disarmament to local congregations. There are many good books and study guides already available; this is not meant to duplicate these. Rather, this book is designed to help people make peacemaking and active concern about the arms race an integral part of the life of a community of faith. It is intended to be a practical book: a book of suggestions and a compilation of ideas for worship, education, and action by people and communities of faith.

This is not a cookbook or an instruction manual for peace work in your church or synagogue. What works in one place may fail in another. Rather, let these ideas spur your own imagination and creativity as you attempt to bring the "good news of peace" to your religious community.

Peacemaking requires courage and creativity. It also requires faith. It is hoped that this book will stir its readers to draw from the depths of their own faith commitments, for it is from the fount of faith that work for peace in the religious community can and should flow. In being faithful, the religious communities will come to respond to the command to "seek peace and pursue it" (Psalm 34:14) and the call to be "makers of peace" (Matthew 5:9).

"If we assume [hu]mankind has a right to survive, then we must find an alternative to war and destruction. In a day when sputniks dash through outer space and guided ballistic missiles are carving highways of death through the stratosphere, nobody can win a war. The choice today is no longer between violence and nonviolence. It is either nonviolence or non-existence.

I am convinced that the Church cannot remain silent while [hu]mankind faces the threat of being plunged into the abyss of nuclear annihilation. If

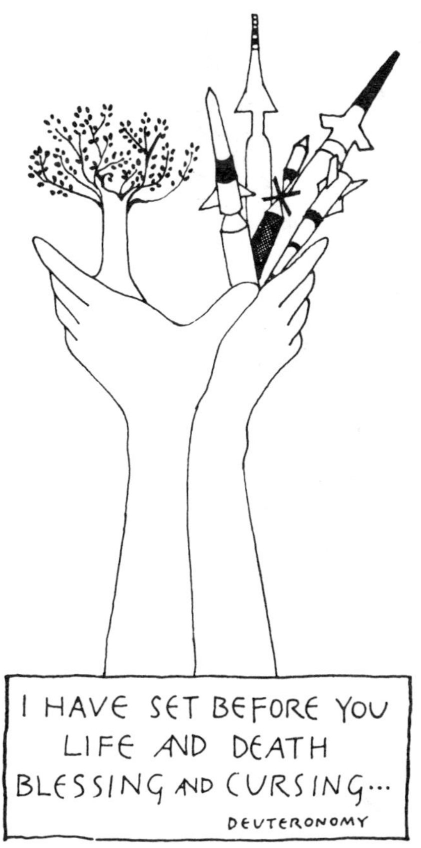

the church is to remain true to its mission, it must call for an end to the arms race."

Martin Luther King, Jr., 1960

This is a critical juncture for the religious communities, a time full of temptation and challenge. The temptation is to retreat from the world, ignoring the complex and frightening issues of war and peace, and to deal exclusively with those very real personal and inter-personal problems which afflict so many people today. The challenge is to respond forthrightly to the arms race and militarism from the depths of the community's faith, incorporating peacemaking and opposition to the arms race in its total life. This temptation and challenge are summed up in the words from the Torah: ". . .I have set before you life and death, blessing and curse; therefore, choose life, that you and your descendants may live." (Deuteronomy 30:19).

"There are many who hate war and who are opposed to peacetime conscription who do not know what they can do, who have no sense of united effort, and who will sit back and accept with resignation the evils which are imposed upon us. This is not working for God's will to be done on earth as it is in Heaven. This is accepting the evils in the world as inevitable and looking toward Heaven as a haven, a "pie in the sky" attitude. God did not make the evils, but man [sic] in his misuse of his free will."

Dorothy Day, 1940

1. Peacemaking: An Integral Dimension of the Life of Faith

The job of the peacemaker is to stop war, to purify the world, to get it saved from poverty and riches, to heal the sick, to comfort the sad, to wake up those who have not yet found God, to create joy and beauty wherever you go, to find God in everything and in everyone.

Muriel Lester

Peacemaking must be a vital part of the life of faith for individuals and for congregations. The value of peace is affirmed in the writings and traditions of all religions. In the *Talmud, Shalom* is a name of God. In the New Testament, Paul calls Jesus "our Peace". And the first of the Five Precepts of Buddhism is not to kill or to be party to the taking of human life.

But all too often the tradition is ignored in practice. The challenge today is to reclaim that tradition, to make peacemaking an integral part of all religious life, and to make this concern explicit and active in the daily lives of communities of faith.

For this purpose, it is important first to consider the meaning of "peace." All too often this word has been used to justify war and violence or to excuse injustice and oppression. Calls for "peace with honor" and pleas against "disturbing the peace" have come from political leaders and others who have tolerated massive violence and oppression. The fullness of the meaning of "peace" must be restored.

The Hebrew word for peace is *shalom*, which literally means "to be whole or integrated." The English word "peace" is derived from the Latin, meaning "making a pact." But the Jewish concept of peace is not so limited to the cessation of war. As George Foot Moore defined it, *shalom* also stands for "Welfare of every kind, sound health, prosperity, contentment, and the like."

This meaning of peace was echoed in a statement of the world's Catholic bishops in 1965 at the Second Vatican Council:

> Peace is not merely the absence of war. Nor can it be reduced to the maintenance of a balance of power between enemies. Nor is it brought about by dictatorship. Indeed, it is rightly called "an enterprise of justice." (Is. 32:7) Peace results from that harmony built into human society by its divine Founder, and actualized by people as they thirst after ever greater justice.

This vision of peace joined with justice is central to biblical *shalom*: peace based on the right relation of the people of God with their God and with each other and, in fact, with the whole of creation. The vision is not only

that swords are beaten into plowshares (Isaiah 2:1-5; Micah 4:1-5) but also that people are secure under their own vines and fig trees (Micah 4:5) and that even traditional enemies, such as the lion and the lamb, will live together in harmony (Isaiah 11:6-9). The consequence of such a vision was noted in the 1980 statement of the United Presbyterian Church, *Peacemaking: The Believers' Calling:*

> The classical biblical image for peacemaking is the turning of swords into plowshares. . .The making of swords and the making of plowshares are two different functions and imply different lifestyles. Swordmaking is for the purpose of defense or aggression. It is actively directed against the enemy real or imagined. Plowmaking is for nurture, for new growth, and ultimately harvest. It is the essential creative activity that makes sustenance of life possible. It is also the activity through which productivity makes possible the inclusion of other people in new community, potential and promising.

Thus, peacemaking, though initially concerned with the elimination of war, includes the wider concerns of nurturing human community and promoting justice. The peacemaker, therefore, is one who shows that promotion of justice and of the peaceful community is an important task in the search to end war.

Peacemaking is also the work of reconciling, of bridging gaps between peoples: between women and men, between poor and rich, between black and white, between Soviet and American. Those promoting justice

4

and peace must not only seek to break down the barriers of fear and mistrust between their own and other nations, helping, for example, Americans to recognize that Soviet citizens are human. But peacemakers must also find ways to reconcile themselves with their adversaries, with those who promote or support military policies. In particular, this means finding ways to help those involved in war preparations — whether as soldiers, politicians, managers or workers in military industries — to question the arms race and their reliance on weapons for defense.

Ultimately, this means that peacemaking is the work of nonviolence. It is the attempt to find alternatives to killing, to violent conflict, and to threats of mass destruction. This is, in a sense, the struggle to "overcome evil with good" (Romans 12:21); for, as *The Dhammapada*, one of the Buddhist scriptures, puts it:

> Anger must be overcome by absence of anger;
> Evil must be overcome by good;
> Greed must be overcome by liberality;
> Lies must be overcome by truth.

Active nonviolence, which must be at the heart of peacemaking, is such an attempt. As people seek to eliminate nuclear weapons and bring peace, they must be concerned not only with the vision but with the means by which they seek to bring this vision into reality. A.J. Muste noted, "There is no way to peace; peace is the way." Gandhi and many others have insisted that peacemakers must be as mindful of the means they use as they are insistent on the ends they seek, for we have control over the means we use but have almost no control over the end.

Peacemaking in the fullest sense is, then, the work of ending war, promoting justice, reconciling enemies, and living and acting nonviolently.

In the past, peacemaking in this sense has taken many forms within the religious communities.

There have always been those who stood up courageously for peace even in the face of opposition and persecution. Francis of Assisi, Catherine of Siena, Menno Simons, George Fox, Mary Dyer, Lucretia Mott, Muriel Lester, Abraham Joshua Heschel, Martin Luther King Jr., Lanza del Vasto, and Dorothy Day are a few of the women and men who have challenged their fellow believers to face the hard questions about injustice, militarism, and war.

Some denominations have publicly expressed a peace witness, especially the historic peace churches: the Mennonites, the Society of Friends (Quakers), and the Church of the Brethren.

Other denominations have long had national boards or offices which have dealt seriously with peace issues, often as part of their other international concerns, producing educational materials and seeking to influence the beliefs of their members and the policies of the country. And especially in the past few decades an outpouring of concern for peace and disarmament has been expressed in statements from national offices and in resolutions adopted at national meetings.

But more seems to be needed. Speaking about his denomination, Charles Cesaretti, the Episcopal Church's Public Issues Officer, noted,

> Episcopalians must come to realize that disarmament and peace will not be achieved by merely passing resolutions. The Episcopal Church has affirmed every disarmament conference since it supported Tsar Nicholas II of Russia's call for a peace conference in 1898. It is a time for commitment, leadership, and risk.

Such commitment has emerged in many religious communities at the national and regional levels. And there have been some major efforts at peacemaking at the local level.

These efforts must be continued but should be supplemented by more intensive work at the congregational level in pursuit of grass roots support for disarmament. This requires religious peacemakers to ask themselves some serious questions, such as those posed by

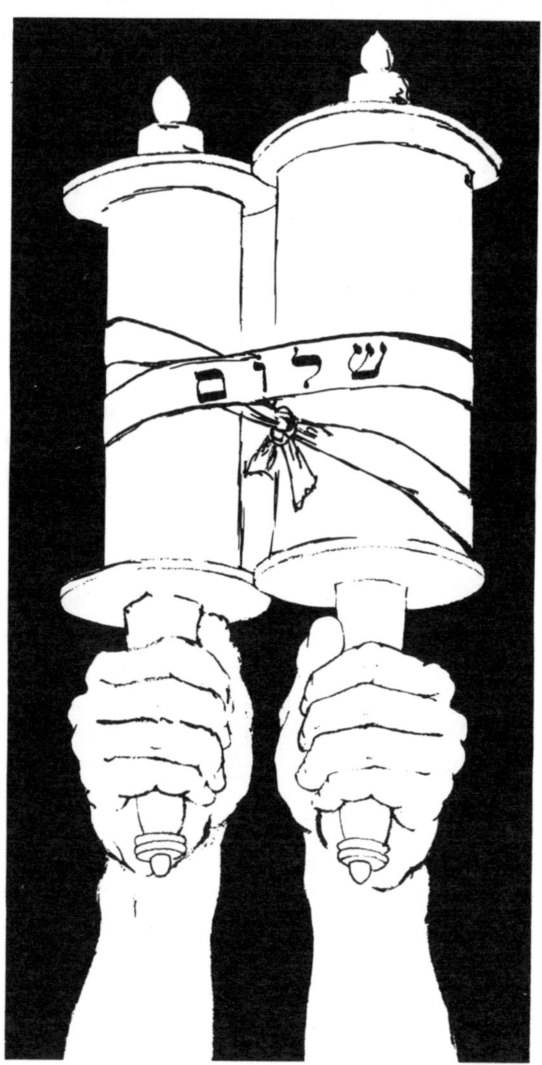

the Rev. Richard Watts at the first Nuclear Weapon Freeze Strategy Conference:

- Is our activity rooted in the church's [or temple's] resources, its tradition, its language?
- Does our work take the parish seriously?
- Are we constantly trying to reach the uncommitted?

It is essential to find ways to make peace central to the lives of local congregations. Peacemaking is not just one more concern which we ask the church or temple to support, as it might support a hunger walk, a Scouting week, or even some piece of national or local legislation. Peace is not just a program concern vying with other programs, but it should become an integral part of the life of faith for a local congregation, permeating its worship, education, and action.

Recently hunger has changed from a "concern" and a "program" of many congregations into a sign of the faithfulness of that congregation. Such a transformation needs to occur with peace. Just as a local church or synagogue should be known by its nurturance of the spiritual lives of its members and by its commitment to the poor and hungry, so should it be known by its peacemaking.

Many congregations are far from integrating peacemaking into their life of faith. It thus becomes important that those who seek to involve people in peacemaking do so with sensitivity to the faith and life of the local community. Peacemakers should be as aware of persons they are working with as of the issues they are confronting. Speaking *with* people and listening to them is an initial concern of the sensitive peacemaker. Speaking *at* people, even for the most noble cause, may end up as speaking to the wind.

In this work, it is sometimes helpful to focus activities on a certain aspect of the issue of peace. Rather than asking people to look at all the issues, ranging from non-violence to world community, concentrating on one issue (e.g., the nuclear weapon freeze or the impact of military spending on the poor) can be an easier way to reach people. Peacemakers ought to plan carefully what they intend to do, not only in regard to what issues they hope to bring up and the style of their presentations, but also in terms of what goals — long range and short term — they hope to accomplish. This can increase effectiveness and help one avoid becoming overwhelmed by all the issues.

Since such peace work in a local congregation is often a difficult and lonely endeavor, interfaith peace groups in a local community can be a source of inspiration and mutual support. These groups can serve as educational forums for religious leaders and others in a community where people can meet to discuss issues and approaches for peacemaking. Or they can promote and plan city or area-wide interfaith events. The Louisville, Kentucky,

Council on Religion and Peacemaking, for example, has sponsored local programs, provided clergy with information, and helped local congregations in programs and prayer services for peace.

In other parts of the country, clergy have sat down at weekly meetings to study the arms race and congregations have joined together for peace activities. Many interfaith peace groups have sponsored major observances with day-long programs of speakers, workshops, and worship services. These and other interfaith efforts for peace are important since they express the unity of religious response in the face of nuclear weapons, war, and oppression. They help provide sustenance for the lonely peace worker in an apathetic or hostile congregation. But they are perhaps even more important in informing, challenging, and supporting people who may afterwards attempt to begin peace work in their separate temples or churches.

The next three chapters offer specific suggestions for integrating peace concerns in the worship, education, and action programs of individual congregations. The interfaith dimension of peacework will supplement this. But it is in the local congregation that possibly the most difficult, yet the most significant, work for peace should be done.

We make peace, we help bring about world peace, if we make peace wherever we are destined and summoned to do so: in the active life of one's community and in that aspect of it which can actively determine its relationship to another community. The prophecy of peace addressed to Israel is not valid only for the days of the coming of the Messiah...Fulfillment in a "then" is inextricably bound up with fulfillment in the "now."

Martin Buber

2. Peacemaking, Prayer, and Worship

Let us forever remember that the sense for the sacred is as vital as the light of the sun. There can be no nature without spirit, no world without the Torah, . . .no humanity without attachment to God.

Abraham Joshua Heschel

The work of peace is a work in the world but rooted in the spirit. Thus cultivation of the spiritual life is a necessary first step in preparing to work for peace in religious communities. And, insofar as religious communities express their faith in corporate worship, peace concerns should be reflected in the services of local churches and synagogues. This chapter begins with a few reflections on the relation of prayer and peacemaking on the personal level and within the life of a worshipping community. These are followed by specific suggestions for incorporating peace concerns in congregational worship.

Prayer and the Peacemaker

In all our acts of resistance, we are
brought back to the need for a deeper
basis, or for a rock outside the world
on which to stand. The deeper question
in the face of our government's violence
was not one of becoming more effective
against it but of reaching the inner
point out of which one could respond more
fully, more deeply, more unitedly, to the
visible and invisible nature of evil.

James Douglass

Working for peace is not easy. The pervasiveness of militarism and of support for violent solutions to international problems demands much patience and persistence from those who oppose the drift toward war. Working for months, even years, without visible results can be extremely demoralizing. The gravity of the world situation can overwhelm people, rendering some of them cynical, some passive, some violent. Thus, those who work for peace need to cultivate a strong personal basis for their lives. Those who seek to make peace in the world must see that they themselves are truly peacemakers. Otherwise, as Thomas Merton once noted,

He [sic] who attempts to act and do things for others
or for the world without deepening his own self-
understanding, freedom, integrity, and capacity to
love will have nothing to give to others. He will
communicate nothing but the contagion of his own
obsession, his ego-centered ambitions, his delusions
about ends and means.

To counter such a temptation, spiritual preparation for peacemaking and a deepening of one's spiritual life

are important first steps. These can provide a healthy antidote to the obsessiveness and violence of contemporary culture which can also affect our ways of peacemaking.

Spiritual preparation for action has been an important aspect of the lives of great religious leaders, reformers, and peacemakers. For example, at critical points in their ministries, Moses, Elijah, Jesus, Paul and many others withdrew to desert places to fast and pray. Gandhi, too, stressed the need for spiritual discipline as a preparation for nonviolent action. Many of the most influential peacemakers made prayer and contemplation central to their lives. Consider the example of Muriel Lester and Dorothy Day in our century.

Many peace activists have also seen that they must not only be spiritually prepared for action but that their actions must be infused by a spirit of prayer. Otherwise the temptation is to become totally absorbed by one's work.

Many religious traditions have developed or encouraged practices that help preserve serenity in the midst of activity. These include the Quaker practice of "centering down," the repetition of "mantras" in various religions (including the "Jesus prayer" of the Eastern Orthodox tradition), and what Brother Lawrence called the "practice of the presence of God." The Vietnamese Buddhist monk Thich Nhat Hanh has offered suggestions of ways to make oneself more aware of what one is doing. For example, he writes:

Wash the dishes relaxingly, as though each bowl
is an object of contemplation. Consider each bowl
as sacred. Follow your breath to prevent your mind

from straying. Do not try to hurry to get the job over with. Consider washing the dishes the most important thing in life. Washing the dishes is meditation. If you cannot wash the dishes in mindfulness, neither can you meditate while sitting in silence.[1]

These and other practices are useful ways to calm and center the self, to pull yourself together when tempted to distraction, and to become more aware of the workings of God.

Busy peaceworkers should occasionally take time out for themselves — times for quiet, reflection, and re-creation. Gandhi spent one day a week in silence. Thich Nhat Hanh suggests taking a day off a month for quiet. Henri Nouwen recommends giving a day a week to God, in silence, meditation, and fasting. Some time spent by yourself, away from daily concerns, can be most refreshing.

Recently some people have urged a return to fasting, for example, on Hiroshima and Nagasaki days (August 6 and 9) . Archbishop Raymond Hunthausen of Seattle has asked Catholics in his diocese to pray and fast each Monday in the face of the nuclear arms race. But this ancient discipline is being revived not merely as an act of repentance for the arms race and a means of spiritual cleansing. Fasting is now seen as a symbolic act of solidarity with the poor, for as the Vatican wrote to the United Nations in 1976, "even when they are not used, by their cost alone, armaments kill the poor by causing them to starve."

Many other aspects of the spiritual life could be mentioned. Search your tradition; read some of the books, both ancient and modern, on prayer. Find ways to cultivate the spiritual dimensions of your own life. Muriel Lester once said:

If we bet our lives on eternity, believing, as Emerson put it, not what the hours say but what the centuries whisper, we shall soon find ourselves facing those who occupy the seats of temporal power and facing them with a sureness of touch. The question then will not be our denomination or 'faith'. It will be how much consciousness of God we have been pure enough in heart to achieve.

Such a consciousness of God and an awareness of all that is can be a means of nurturing hope in us. In the words of Henri Nouwen,

When we have lost the vision, we have nothing to show; when we have forgotten the Word of God, we have nothing to remember; when we have buried the blueprint of our life, we have nothing to build. But when we keep in touch with the life-giving spirit within us, we can lead people out of their captivity and become hope-giving guides.[2]

---

1. *The Miracle of Mindfulness*, p. 85.
2. Henri Nouwen, *The Living Reminder*, p. 73.

Corporate Worship and Peace

The personal life of prayer and reflectiveness demands something more. The Quaker writer, Douglas Steere, wrote that "we need corporate encouragement to recall and to be re-dedicated to that deep citizenship to which our lives stand pledged."

Some form of corporate worship is the central act of most religions. Public worship is an acknowledgment by a community of faith of the holy, of the dimension of life beyond the ordinary. The expressions of this vary from the silence and simplicity of a Friends meeting to the music and majesty of an Orthodox liturgy to the energy and enthusiasm of a revival meeting. In all of these, there is a recognition that the worshipping community derives its identity from its relation to another dimension of reality.

Since worship is so central, it should reflect the centrality of peacemaking to religion. Therefore, if peacemaking is truly integral to a community of faith, its worship should reflect this concern. Peace will not only be mentioned in prayers of intercession or in sermons but even the way people worship will manifest peace. Worship will acknowledge that spiritual life and faith are not means to escape from the world. Rather, worship will empower the community to make real that vision of peace which is at the heart of true religion.

Worship will then be an expression of hope for the world and for the people who come together to pray.

Worship may also be a sign of the resistance of the community to the contemporary militarism, injustice, and reliance on violence. Worship can be that act of a community that says clearly that its values are not determined by public opinion or by governmental ideology. As Jim Wallis wrote in the March 1979 *Sojourners*, "Prayer is the act of reclaiming our identity as children of God. Prayer declares who we are and to whom we belong. . . Prayer is acting upon who we really are and thus has the effect of dismantling the illusions that have controlled us."

But how can our worship express this? The degree and the manner in which peacemaking permeates the worship life of any local congregation depends on many factors, not least of all the degree of that congregation's commitment to peace.

This chapter includes some suggestions for incorporating peace in worship services. But keep a few things in mind while attempting this:

Be sensitive to the traditions and styles of worship of a congregation. All styles of worship can reflect the congregation's concern for peace. It would be a serious mistake to have one style become identified with peace. Peace can be sung about in folk style hymns and in venerable hymn tunes.

Be hopeful in worship. A worship filled with despair or one that emphasizes only the evils of the world may only enhance people's feelings of powerlessness and despair.

19.

Worship should add something to life and reflect the realization that people of faith do not look to governments or even to daily newspapers for their vision of reality. Faith offers hope and a vision not limited to the way things are.

And *let your worship be a celebration.* Even in the face of the forces of death, your worship as peacemakers should affirm life. In the midst of recognizing the pervasiveness of evil and death in the world, peacemakers should acknowledge the possibility of repentance, of forgiveness, of new life. For people of faith are not purveyors of bad news. They are called upon to expose evil and condemn destructiveness because they are advocates of life (Deuteronomy 30:20) and because they are dreamers of dreams (Joel 2:28-29). This can be done especially in corporate prayer. In Jim Wallis' words, "Rather than merely criticizing the idolatrous authorities responsible for the evil, prayer radically asserts what our higher authority is. In recognizing God's authority, prayer moves us beyond opposition to affirmation, beyond resistance to celebration."

Finally, *make your worship an act of reconciling love.* Acknowledging your relationship with God, recognize also the presence of God in your midst and in your relationships with others. Worship should be a way of reconciling us with others, praying for enemies and adversaries, reaching out to those whom you have injured and who have injured you. Worship should especially be informed by the intention of making community, finding ways for those who seriously disagree to worship together, despite their differences.

Suggestions for Incorporating Peace in Worship

The task of making peace central to the worship life of a congregation may be easy. You may merely have to ask those responsible for worship to incorporate peace concerns in services. If you are not a member of the clergy or of a worship committee, approach them expressing your concern, eliciting their interest and support, and offering suggestions and assistance. You may have to be gently persistent in this if there is no immediate response.

Once you begin planning worship, be both creative and traditional. Many resources are available, especially those from your own denomination. Worship books often provide services, responsive readings, intercessory prayers, and other materials on peace and justice. Many hymns, when used in conjunction with certain readings and other worship resources, can bring forth peace themes in quite unusual and unexpected ways. In addition, many denominations provide worship materials for special days (World Order Sunday, World Day of Prayer for Peace, Peace Sabbath).

But be creative. Use symbols, from breaking of bread and greetings of peace to collection of war toys and offerings of food for the hungry. Light candles for peace. Symbols can open up new dimensions of reality. Also try integrating prayers and styles of worship from other cultures into your worship as a way of internationalizing liturgy. This is especially appropriate when praying for the oppressed in other lands.[3]

Peace in Worship Services

There are many different elements of a worship service which offer opportunities for incorporating peace concerns.

Readings: Many worship services use readings. Many biblical passages speak poignantly of peace and justice.[4] Select readings carefully, being especially sensitive to how the readings relate to each other and to the other parts of the service. In those denominations which use a lectionary, many of the assigned readings are pertinent to peace concerns.

Explore the use of nonscriptural materials, either as supplements or substitutes for scriptural readings. A contemporary paraphrase of a scripture passage can be very enlightening.[5] Poems, short readings, and dramatic readings are also good. Eyewitness accounts of the bombings of Hiroshima and Nagasaki are very moving and can be effectively combined with scriptural readings.[6] Other accounts of war, injustice, and oppression might be appropriate on occasion. Construct a reading which

3. Ideas for diversifying worship can be found in Goff, *In Every Person Who Hopes*, and Gonzalez, *In Accord: Let Us Worship.*
4. See Ronald J. Sider, *Cry Justice: The Bible on Hunger and Poverty.*
5. For example, Dan Berrigan's *Uncommon Prayer*, Clarence Jordan's *Cotton Patch Versions* of New Testament Books, Ernesto Cardenal's *Psalms*, and Peter Ediger's paraphrases (some of which appeared in *God and Caesar* newsletter, CHM, Box 347, Newton, KS 67114).
6. Accounts of Hiroshima and Nagasaki can be obtained in books from Wilmington College Peace Resource Center, Pyle Center, Box 1183, Wilmington, Ohio 45177. See also *Fellowship* July/August, 1980, *Atlantic Monthly* August, 1980, and *The Progressive* August, 1981. A slide show of paintings of Hiroshima victims, *Unforgettable Fire*, can be rented from CALC ($7.00 fee). You might also use the Proceedings of the National Citizens Hearings for Radiation Victims, *Invisible Violence*, available from the FOR or National Committee for Radiation Victims, 317 Pennsylvania Ave. SE, Washington, D.C. 20003. ($2.50 each)

alternates between newspaper headlines and scriptural passages.

<u>Music</u>: Singing is a way for people to express their deepest emotions and simultaneously to promote a feeling of unity among those singing. Songs can be inspiring, cathartic, unifying, Look carefully for hymns that express peace and justice themes directly or express other related themes (such as reliance on God for security). Try adapting some hymns which might be non-inclusive in their language or which utilize too-militaristic metaphors. Look for new hymns and revised versions of hymns which express these concerns more effectively than the old translations.[7]

Many spirituals (especially "Down by the Riverside") and Jewish songs (especially "Vine and Fig Tree" and "Shalom Chaverim") are appropriate. Many of the more recent folk hymns have justice and peace themes (including the works of the Weston monks). Try using some of the many folk songs and traditional peace songs (as well as popular songs). Finally, there are anthems and hymns for choirs which evoke peace themes.[8]

<u>Prayers</u>: Introduce peace and justice concerns in the prayers of a service. Prayers of repentance are ways to remind ourselves that we, too, are responsible for continuing violence and injustice in the world. They help remind us what Andre Trocme once wrote:

> ...the church, possessing as it does the secret of repentance and faith, cannot maintain as Peter did when they were killing his neighbor, "I don't know the man." It is for Christians [and for all people of faith] of all countries to repent first on their own account, and to change their conduct without delay."

For then, as Merton suggested, "Only when we have become able to accept the basic contradictions in our own self can we have the humility to understand the contradictions in others and in society."

Intercessory prayers are a most appropriate place to mention peace and justice issues and to pray for the victims of violence and oppression. Prayer for others can bring us closer to them. It is a way to reach out to others near and far, and especially to our enemies. As Rabbi Yehiel Mikhal, the eighteenth century Hassidic master, said, "Pray for enemies that all may be well with them. And should you think this is not serving God, rest assured that more than all prayers, this is, indeed, the service of God."

Other prayers in a service may also reflect peace concerns. Use ones in your denominational prayer book, compose your own, or leave room for spontaneous prayer.

<u>Silence</u>: Silence in a worship service can be a way of calming people, of promoting reflectiveness (especially

Altar reconstructed from burnt timbers and bombed stones at Coventry Cathedral in England.

after a poignant reading), and of promoting a peaceful atmosphere for worship. Time for silence can also be an antidote to the noisiness of our busy and all too violent world.

<u>Sermons</u>: The spoken word, coming from a rabbi, minister, priest, or lay preacher, can be the most effective way of spreading the message of peace in a worship service. The speaker can help a congregation reflect on current world events and important moral issues in the light of faith. The pulpit has been the place where some have continued the work of the prophets by denouncing injustice, confronting violence, and calling for peace.[9]

In more biblically oriented congregations, a preacher might find it best to expound on the meaning of a scriptural passage and show how this relates to all aspects of life, from the personal and family lives of the members of the congregation to the life of the family of nations. The challenge here will be to show how peace and justice (and action for these) are integral to the life of faith.

Others might want to start from a current event, try to explore its meaning, and then reflect on its moral ramifications. A knowledge of the denomination's traditions and recent resolutions is helpful.

Others may find that people in their congregation are receptive to other styles of preaching, which might be more prophetic in tone or which might be an ethical reflection on events. In all cases, the speaker must be sensitive to the congregation.

---

7. An example is Omer Westendorff's version of "A Mighty Fortress is Our God" from the World Library of Sacred Music.

8. Some selected musical selections are listed at the end of this chapter.

9. Sample sermons are found in the Peace Sabbath packets and in the Blue Book series available from Riverside Church Disarmament Program, in the *Clergy Resource Guide* of the Interfaith Center to Reverse the Arms Race, and in the collection *An Alternative of Grace* (Presbyterian Distribution Service, Room 935, 475 Riverside Drive, New York, NY 10115. $1.00). See also Ronald Sider and Darrel Brubaker, ed., *Preaching on Peace* (Fortress, $3.95).

Sometimes the congregation's religious leader might not be willing to preach a peace sermon but might be open to have someone else speak and thus "test the waters." A pulpit exchange might be arranged in which one or both clergy speak on peace. Local people, even members of the congregation, who are articulate in the religious basis of their peacemaking, might be persuaded to preach one week. Some visiting lecturers are also willing to speak at worship services.[10] And a local peace group might make speakers available for churches or temples.[11]

Sermons obviously need to be prepared carefully. They should be ways to lead people to commitment to peacemaking. They are meant to challenge people and confront them with the issues in light of faith, but without alienating them unduly. This, of course, depends largely on the speaker's personal style and on how the message is presented. Political issues must be handled delicately and accurately. Presenting issues in the light of faith can help undercut the charge that one is "politicizing" religion. In some congregations, there may be a need to prepare people for sermons on peace by first of all explaining the relation of faith and politics.

There are ways to handle even the most controversial topic and yet not completely alienate a congregation. Sometimes people need to feel that the speaker is concerned about them personally. Sometimes people only need to let off steam. Consider having a discussion period on the sermon immediately after the service. A more daring preacher might invite questions during the service itself. One pastor who had given a highly controversial sermon distributed copies of it and invited people to come to a discussion a few weeks later. This helped ease some of the tensions in the congregation which might have resulted in the loss of his pastorate.

It is sometimes necessary to risk controversy and, in fact, controversy is bound to occur if one speaks forthrightly for peace. The prophets, Jesus, and many other religious leaders were often not accepted by those who heard them. Many have suffered and died for their outspokenness. Today the most that many in the U.S. have to fear is loss of their jobs. Preachers, speakers, and pastors must be aware of this and develop the inner spiritual resources and moral support to help deal with these problems.

Miscellaneous: There are many other ways to bring the peace issue into worship services. Greetings of peace and reconciliation manifest the need for unity. In litanies and responsive readings, people can share concerns for justice. The time for announcements might include a period for recalling some of the evils which had occurred in the past week. (In Nazi Germany, the Confessing Church often mentioned disappearances in services; in El Salvador, Archbishop Romero mentioned the names of those who had been killed the previous week.)

Audio-visuals (films and slide shows) and recorded songs can enhance a service. Colorful banners, joyful processions, and clowns and puppets can be non-threatening ways to promote peace.

It is often good, as part of a service, to include acts of commitment. These might be individual commitments, signed pledges, offerings of letters on an issue (to be sent to governmental authorities), covenant agreements, or even the whole congregation's commitment to peacemaking activities.

And special collections for the hungry present an opportunity to show the links between the arms race and hunger.

Peace Services

A real challenge is to design a complete service or series of services around peacemaking themes. Some possible themes are: peace, the disarmed life, personal nonviolence, ministry of reconciliation; repentance for Hiroshima and Nagasaki, for racism, or for the Holocaust; disarmament, the arms race and the poor, fueling the arms race abroad, the idolatry of the bomb, swords into plowshares, respecting the earth; pacifism, nuclear pacifism, the just war and the bomb; and prophetic peacemakers. Find a theme and then design a service or series of services around it. All the parts of the services, from the opening words to the closing prayers, would explore that theme.

Using a theme as the basis of worship can be adapted to many styles of worship. A few Quakers in London come together once a month for a special meeting for worship for the tortured and their torturers. An interfaith service for peace at the time of the first United Nations Special Session on Disarmament incorporated elements from many faiths (including Shinto, Buddhist, Muslim, Jewish. and Christian), concluded with a Community Affirmation, and was followed by a march to the United Nations.

There are many times when it is especially appropriate to incorporate peace concerns in the worship of a congregation.

Use the opportunities present in the religious calendar. If there is a lectionary for your denomination, the suggested readings are the obvious place from which to start designing a peace service for that week.

Special holy days also suggest peace themes. Yom Kippur is a day Jews call for repentance; perhaps repentance for social sin (injustice, preparation for war, etc.) could be included in prayers and reflections. Ash Wednesday is a day of Christian penance beginning the season of Lent; it has often been used by groups to call to mind the evils of war and injustice. The seasons of Advent and Christmas in which many scripture readings speak of

---

peace, are also obvious occasions to make specific the meaning of peace today. Passover is the Jewish celebration of liberation from the slavery of Egypt. Many Jewish and interfaith groups have celebrated special Seder meals or services on the themes of freedom, justice, and peace.[12] Many Christian groups have gathered on Good Friday to show parallels between Jesus' sufferings and current suffering by people throughout the world. A public "Stations of the Cross" might stop at nuclear weapons facilities, draft boards or recruiting stations, embassies or consulates of oppressive regimes, federal buildings, banks supporting red-lining or apartheid, hospitals where the poor are badly treated, run-down housing and schools, and other places, praying for those who now suffer and calling those present to commit themselves to work for justice and peace. These are only a few ways to use seasons of the year and feasts creatively.

______________COMMUNITY AFFIRMATION______________

We, who live in the shadow of the mushroom cloud,
We, whose very bones and lungs are threatened
*   even now by radioactivity,*
Today declare our hope in the future.

From the diversity of our religious traditions,
We have come to renew our belief in the holiness of
*   the earth and the sanctity of all life.*

We declare we are at peace with all people of good
*   will.*
We need no leader to define for us any enemy,
Nor to tell us what we need security for and defense
*   against.*

Instead, we affirm that our earth's security rests not
*   in armaments, but*
In the justice of adequate housing and food,
In the justice of meaningful education and work,
In the justice of an economic order that gives every-
*   one access to our earth's abundance,*
In the justice of human relationships, nourished by
*   cooperation,*
In the justice of safe, clean and renewable energy,
*   instead of the perils of nuclear power.*

We affirm people over property, community over
*   privatism,*
Respect for others regardless of sex, race or class.

We choose struggle rather than indifference,
We choose to be friends of the earth and of one
*   another, rather than exploiters.*
We choose to be citizens rather than subjects,
We choose to be peacemakers rather than peace-
*   keepers,*

We choose a nuclear-free future,
And we will settle for nothing less.

We unite ourselves with sisters and brothers the
*   world over,*
To join together in communities of resistance to the
*   nuclear threat.*
We unite ourselves with trust in the Spirit of Life;
Justice and love can overcome the machines of
*   destruction.*

Before us today are set life and death,
We choose life, that we and our children may live.
Let it be so.

____

Many religious bodies have designated certain days for peace. These include World Order Sunday (the Sunday near October 24, the date of the founding of the United Nations) in many Protestant denominations and the World Day of Peace (usually January 1) in Catholic churches. Some interfaith groups have also called for special times of concern for peace. Peace Sabbath begun by Riverside Church in 1979 is now co-sponsored by the Fellowship of Reconciliation, Clergy and Laity Concerned, and the Religious Task Force. The weekend after Easter and Passover was the suggested date of this observance from 1979 to 1981, though different local and regional religious bodies have used other dates.[13] Since 1979, Sojourners Peace Ministry has encouraged people to spend Memorial Day as a day of prayer for peace and of remembrance of what nuclear war means. In 1982, Sojourners joined as a co-sponsor of Peace Sabbath which was held on Memorial Day weekend which in that year included the Christian feast of Pentecost and the Jewish festival of Shavuoth.[14] Several groups in this country and abroad have also designated the week around October 24 (the founding of the United Nations) as a Week of Prayer for Peace.

There are other special days on which groups could gather for prayer. January 15 is the birthday of Martin Luther King, Jr., the nonviolent advocate of social justice, peace, and the end to racism and oppression. An interfaith service bringing together people from divergent religious, cultural, and racial backgrounds would be a most pertinent tribute.[15] April 15 is Tax Day, a day to remember that over half of U.S. tax money goes for war rather than peace. October 24 is the anniversary of the founding of the United Nations. December 10 is Human Rights Day, the anniversary of the U.N. declaration of the rights of all peoples.[16]

____

12. In the late sixties, Arthur Waskow wrote a *Freedom Seder*, combining the traditional elements of the Seder with readings and reflections from civil rights advocates. More recently, he has prepared a *Shalom Seder*. See Resource List at the end of this chapter.

____

13. Peace Sabbath packets, including sample sermons, a poster, and liturgical aids, are available from the co-sponsoring groups.
14. Contact FOR for details.
15. A packet of resources on Martin Luther King, Jr. is available from FOR.
16. A copy of the Universal Declaration of Human Rights, incorporating scriptural passages and statements from various denominations is available from the U.S. Catholic Conference Division for Latin America, P.O. Box 6060, Washington, DC 20005. (50¢)

August 6 and 9, the anniversaries of the bombings of Hiroshima and Nagasaki, are the most appropriate times for special observances. These days should become special occasions to renew commitments to work to abolish nuclear weapons. In recent years, many groups have held vigils, services, and demonstrations in these days. Some have adopted traditions from Japan for these services. Making paper cranes has become an activity for children. Groups have floated candle lanterns on lakes and rivers in the evening of August 6. (In Hiroshima, this is done each year as a memorial for the dead, many of whom fled to the river for relief from their burns.) In 1981, a fast was sponsored by several groups (including FOR and American Friends Service Committee [AFSC]) on those days; people fasted to express their concern for the poor, who are the first victims of massive arms spending and to signify their support of a nuclear weapon freeze.

August 6 in the calendar of the Episcopal and Catholic churches is the feast of the Transfiguration when Jesus was glorified and spoke with Moses and Elijah. (Luke 9: 28-36; Mark 9:2-9; Matthew 17:1-9.) The contrast of the light surrounding Jesus with the awful light of the bomb at Hiroshima is an apt symbol for that day.

In 1981, the Jewish day of mourning for the destruction of the Temples — Tisha B'Av — fell on Nagasaki day. New Jewish Agenda urged Jewish groups to combine the traditions of prayer, fasting, and reading of *Eicha* (*Lamentations* of Jeremiah) with special remembrance of the first atomic bombings.[17]

_____________ SAMPLE SERVICE: Aug. 6-9 _____________

Procession (with songs, people carrying paper cranes)

Call to Prayer: Deuteronomy 30:19

Reading from a survivor of the bombing of Hiroshima

Scriptural response: Psalm 60:1-5

Period of silent prayer

Scripture reading: Luke 9:51-56 (including variant readings)

Short readings from selected religious leaders on Hiroshima: e.g., Billy Graham, Abraham Joshua Heschel, Pope Paul VI, Gandhi

Scripture reading: Isaiah 2:1-5

Intercessory Prayers

Prayer of Commitment: St. Francis Peace Prayer

Closing Prayer

(If near a body of water, consider floating candle lanterns)

In these and other ways, people of faith can combine their worship with remembrance of Hiroshima and Nagasaki and commit themselves to active involvement in disarmament work. As Pope John Paul II said at Hiroshima, "To remember Hiroshima is to abhor nuclear war. To remember Hiroshima is to commit oneself to peace."[18]

Many other days in the year are also appropriate occasions, not least of all Mother's Day. On that day in 1981, Women's Party for Survival and other groups gathered in Washington, D.C. and elsewhere to call for disarmament. This was in line with the tradition of the great women peacemakers, Julia Ward Howe and Lucretia Mott, who in 1872 began annual observances of a Mother's Peace Festival.

Often there are international or national events which call for a prayerful response. Many local communities held programs and prayer services before and during the United Nations Second Special Session on Disarmament in June 1982.[19] Another occasion is the Sixth Assembly of the World Council of Churches to be held in Vancouver, BC, Canada, from July 24 to August 10, 1983.[20]

The first anniversary of the death of Archbishop Oscar Romero of El Salvador (March 24, 1980) was a time when many gathered not only to pray for the Archbishop and the other victims of the violence in that country but to express their opposition to U.S. military support of El Salvador. The prayer of the people was a cry to stop oppression.[21]

Groups might hold special services of prayer and worship whenever international violence flares up and whenever any nation tests a nuclear weapon.[22] In these and other ways, prayer can be combined with resistance.

Many events thus suggest possible themes and occasions for praying and worshipping for peace for local congregations or interfaith and ecumenical bodies. The style of these may range from the traditional to the innovative. The place may be a nuclear weapons facility or a cathedral. What is important is that a way will be found to worship as a witness for peace suitable to those involved. This will probably be a combination of the traditional and the innovative.

Combining praying and peacemaking may help re-invigorate the traditions and celebrations of the faith communities involved, making clear both the timelessness and timeliness of religious truth.

17. See *Menorah*, May/June 1981 and Arthur Waskow's *Seasons of Our Joy* (Bantam, $8.95)

18. A Hiroshima kit is available from Interfaith Center to Reverse the Arms Race, containing sample sermons, prayers, quotes, and instructions for making paper cranes. ($2.00)

19. The World Peace Prayer, originally begun as an international effort to pray for this event, is one continuing effort of prayer for peace. Postcards of this prayer, in either English or Spanish, are available from FOR's Covenant Peacemaking program. (10¢ each; 100 or more, 5¢ each; plus 20% shipping). See page 9.

20. For information on these events, contact FOR.

21. Liturgical aids were provided by Interreligious Task Force on El Salvador, 475 Riverside Drive, Room 1020, New York, NY 10115.

22. Citizens Call keeps people informed of U.S. nuclear weapons tests. To become part of their network, send $5.00 to Citizens Call, 1321 East 400 South, Salt Lake City, UT 84102. (FOR's Disarmament Program has a Comprehensive Test Ban packet; cost: $1.00.)

Resources

Prayer

Anthony Bloom, *Beginning to Pray.* (Paulist. $3.95)

William Callahan & Francine Cardman, *The Wind Is Rising: Prayer Ways for Active People.* (Quixote Center, 3311 Chauncey Place, #301, Mt. Rainier, MD 20822)

James W. Douglass, *Lightning East to West.* (Sunburst Press, Box 6, Portland, OR 97215. $4.50) *

Brother Lawrence, *The Practice of the Presence of God.* (Paulist. $2.95)

Thomas Merton, *Contemplation in a World of Action.* (Image Books. $3.95)

Thich Nhat Hanh, *The Miracle of Mindfulness: A Manual on Meditation.* (Beacon. $4.95) *

Henri Nouwen, *Reaching Out: The Three Moments of the Spiritual Life.* (Doubleday. $7.95) *The Way of the Heart: Desert Spiritually and Contemporary Ministry.* (Seabury. $7.95)

Basil Pennington, ed., *Prayer and Liberation.* (Alba. $1.75)

Lanza del Vasto, *Make Straight the Way of the Lord.* (Knopf. $1.75) *

Worship Aids

An Alternative of Grace: Peacemaking Sermons. Vol. 1. (Presbyterian Distribution Service, Room 935, 475 Riverside Drive, New York, NY 10115. $1)

My People, I Am Your Security: Worship Resources in a Nuclear Age. (Sojourners. $2.50)

Daniel Berrigan, *Uncommon Prayer: A Book of Psalms.* (Seabury. $6.95) *

Ernesto Cardenal, *Psalms.* (Crossroads. $3.95)

Regis Duffy, *Real Presence: Worship, Sacraments, and Commitment.* (Harper & Row. $8.95)

John Eagleson & Philip Sharper, *The Patriot's Bible.* (Orbis)

Kenneth & Caroline Freedman, *My Delight Is In Her: Prayers for Peace in Israel.* (Freedman, 6417 Fourth Ave., Tacoma Park, MD 20012)

James & Margaret Goff, *In Every Person Who Hopes.* (Friendship Press. $3.75) *

Justo & Catherine Gonzalez, *In Accord: Let Us Worship.* (Friendship Press. $3.95)

Clarence Jordan, *Cotton Patch Version of Hebrews and General Epistles. Cotton Patch Version of Luke and Acts.* (Association. $3.95) *Cotton Patch Version of Matthew and John.* (Association. $2.95) *Cotton Patch Version of Paul's Epistles.* (Association. $3.95) *Sermon on the Mount.* (Judson. $2.95)

Charles McCarthy, *Stations of the Cross of Nonviolent Love.* (Needham Peace and Justice Center, 238 Harris Avenue, Needham, MA 02192. $1.50)

Ruth Miner, *Days to Celebrate.* (WILPF. $3)* *Supplement of Readings.* (WILPF. $3) *

Ronald Sider, *Cry Justice! The Bible on Poverty and Hunger.* (Paulist. $2.45)

Ronald J. Sider & Darrel J. Brubaker, ed., *Preaching on Peace.* (Fortress. $3.95)

Arthur Waskow, *Freedom Seder.* (Holt, Rinehart, Winston. $1.50) *Seasons of Our Joy: A Handbook of Jewish Festivals.* (Bantam. $8.95) *Shalom Seder.* (Available from Menorah, Public Resource Center, 1747 Connecticut Avenue NW, Washington, DC 20009. $2.50)

Selected Songs and Hymns found in many traditional Christian hymnals:

God of Grace and God of Glory (Harry Emerson Fosdick)
In Christ There is No East or West (John Oxenham)
O God of Earth and Altar (G.K. Chesterton)
O God of Love, O Prince of Peace (Henry Baker)
Peace in Our Time (John Oxenham/Diademata)
This Is My Song (Lloyd Stone/Sibelius)
Thy Kingdom Come, O God (Lewis Hensley)

Selected folk style hymns or songs:

All of Your People (in *Songs of Praise*, Word of God Music, Box 87, Ann Arbor, MI 48107)

Cry of the Poor (St. Louis Jesuits, from North American Liturgy Resources, 2110 W. Peoria Ave., Phoenix, AZ 85029)

Choose Life; Listen; The Beatitudes: Our Peace and Our Integrity. (Weston Priory, Weston, VT 05161)

God gives peace like a river; The Spirit of the Lord (Isaiah 61:1-2). (in *Combined Sounds of Living Water and Fresh Sounds*, Fisherfolk, Box 130, Woodland Park, CO 80863)

Let There Be Peace on Earth (Sy Miller and Jill Jackson)

Peace is Flowing Like a River (Carey Landry, from North American Liturgy Resources)

Prayer of St. Francis. (Sebastian Temple, from World Library of Sacred Music)

To You, Yahweh, I Lift Up My Soul (in *Cry Hosanna*, Hope Publishing Co., Carol Stream, IL 60187)

Other selected songs:

Dona Nobis Pacem (traditional round)
Down by the Riverside
How Can I Keep from Singing?
Last Night I Had the Strangest Dream (Ed McCurdy)
Lo Yisa Goy/Vine and Fig Tree
We Shall Overcome
What Have They Done to the Rain? (Malvina Reynolds)

A peace song book will be available from FOR and CALC in 1983.

---

*Available from FOR; please add 20% for postage & handling.

3. Educating for Peace in the Congregation

There is perhaps only one hope for the future. This is that the people will learn the facts in time, and that an aroused public opinion will force the politicians to gain control, to stop the nuclear arms race, and to reduce armaments . . . The great challenge to all popular movements — political parties, churches, trade unions, and others — is to help inform public opinion and to organize protests against the arms race. We must present the facts about the arms race to the general public in a way that will make people understand what is going on.

Olaf Palme, former Prime Minister of Sweden

A growing number of people today are worried about the arms race. Some of them may become involved in actions for peace, if only peace advocates can reach them in a way they understand. This is the special challenge for peace educators in the religious community in this country.

The local congregation is the primary place in which to begin this effort. Clergy can preach sermons. Special programs can be arranged and study groups formed. Special presentations can be given at the meetings of the many groups associated with the congregation. And interfaith peace meetings can be arranged between two congregations or on a wider regional basis.

Peace education requires creativity, sensitivity, and experimentation. Reach out to people where they are and seek to discover styles of educating that invite people to share your involvement in peacemaking. Effectiveness is dependent on finding ways to articulate peace concerns so others will listen.

First of all, this means reaching out to people and speaking to them in the places where they gather. You cannot expect many people to come out for a peace program unless they are already interested or committed. But a speaker at a meeting of an established group has a greater opportunity to reach the uncommitted. The groups you might approach can be as disparate as the monthly church supper, the local chapter of Church Women United, the Rotary, or even veterans' groups.

When you approach others, seek to speak with them, not *at* them. They may already be concerned about the issue but need some assistance in interpreting the facts and arguments they have heard from others. Try to articulate your message in a clear way that not only explains the issue but also invites others to become involved in serious discussion. Take care to avoid self-righteousness and any impression that you have all the answers. Instead, speak to people's real concerns, values, and fears, and admit your own limitations. Self-righteousness is a sure way to alienate others, but if you honestly present your message and let people know of your overriding concern for the well-being of all people in the face of a dangerous and costly arms race, you are more likely to elicit positive responses from your audiences.

One way to do this is by approaching the issues in terms of values people cherish and concepts they understand. Speaking about imperialism or capitalistic exploitation is not likely to be an effective way to reach a typical congregation. They are more likely to listen if you try to show that a militaristic foreign policy and the arms race are in opposition to such stated national values as "liberty and justice for all" and to such moral and religious values as the sacredness of human life.

You can also help people to see the connections between their daily lives and pervasive militarism. Explaining the economic and social costs of the arms race or detailing the effects of nuclear war are vivid ways to make what may seem to be an abstract issue into something real and concrete.

You can also start your work by identifying with people's present moral concerns. Compassion may be the springboard to peacemaking for these people. Many of those who are concerned about hunger and human rights can be led to see the connections between hunger and the arms race and between repression and foreign military sales.[1]

---

1. See John Nelson's *Hunger for Justice* (Orbis $4.95) and Bread for the World's study guide, *Hunger and Global Security*.

And since faith is at the basis of religion, help people see that reliance on nuclear weapons for security is surely opposed to any true faith in God.

All your educational efforts should be done in a non-adversarial style. Rhetorical argumentations and angry debates may polarize people and prevent them from hearing any facts or arguments. Ultimately, genuine dialogue is the most effective way to help people face the issues of war and peace. In 1953, Martin Buber wrote,

War has an adversary who hardly ever comes forward as such but does his work in the stillness. This adversary is speech, fulfilled speech, the speech of genuine conversation in which men [*sic*] understand one another and come to a mutual understanding.

The goal of peace education is not winning arguments but convincing people about the urgency of peace and involving them in peacemaking. This demands a dialogical approach that cares for the whole person, that works not only for political results but also for inner transformation. So find ways to approach people not only intellectually but also spiritually, emotionally, and psychologically. The whole person, both yourself and the other, must be turned from war to peace.

In your educational work, focusing on a specific issue will help give some clarity to your presentations. Some groups may want to have ongoing educational events that cover a whole range of issues in the course of a few months or years. But you will probably find that an evening program, a speech, and even a study group functions best if it concentrates on addressing one issue. A carefully chosen issue also has the potential of exciting the interest of more than just a few people.

Recognize also that your educational efforts may be slow and painstaking and that you may not see results for a long time. Patience and perseverance are especially important.

Beginning Educational Efforts

Educate yourself.

The first step toward educating others is, of course, to prepare yourself. Before reaching out to others, begin to study the issue. Explore the reasons for your concern and select the issues you believe are most important. Focus on a few issues; study the facts and arguments. In particular, examine the moral, theological, and spiritual issues involved. While studying, look at the issues with an eye toward finding the most effective ways of explaining them to others.

Try to involve others in your initial study. Include friends, members of your congregation, local clergy, people from other congregations, and other members of the community. You might meet regularly to share concerns, study issues, and plan and execute outreach activi-

ties. Those involved may even help provide each other with moral support for their individual peace activities.

Contact clergy.

In seeking to initiate educational efforts in an individual church or temple, you should first contact the clergy or religious leader. (A simple visit may arouse their interest and involvement.) Share your concern with them, explaining why you are involved in peace and, if it seems necessary, what your background is. Ask them to preach a sermon on peace or to arrange a special peace program for the congregation. Offer to plan programs or study groups. And, before you leave, give them some literature and details on how to contact you or your group. A follow-up phone call or letter is often useful.

Organize a program.

If the rabbi or pastor agrees, arrange a program that will attract the interest of members of the congregation. The event might be a special evening educational program, a worship service, or some combination of both. Or you might schedule a discussion immediately after a worship service when people are already gathered together. You might also present something as part of one of the congregation's ongoing educational program.

Many types of programs are possible. Start a discussion with a film or slide show. Bring in a speaker or a panel, or speak yourself. You might persuade a local official or a member of congress or the state legislature to come and speak on an issue such as budget priorities and military spending. Or you might follow the example of one church which held an evening discussion between a local defense plant manager who was a church member and a peace worker employed by the state's ecumenical council.

These programs should spark people's interest, introduce them to the issues, and interest them in further study and even action. So be sure to follow up with any people who seem concerned.

Involve other congregational groups.

In trying to arrange programs in a congregation, also try contacting other groups and persons. Most congregations have governing or advisory boards which have some say in the direction and activities of that congregation. Approach sympathetic board members or speak at one of the board's regular meetings, sharing your concern and asking their support for programs in the congregation.

Many congregations have social justice committees, mission boards, or other groups concerned with peace and justice issues. These may be persuaded to sponsor and help plan programs; they may even decide to make peace one of their group's priorities. An education committee might also welcome input, especially if you are willing to help in some classes. But also approach other congregational groups: adult, senior citizen, and youth groups; bible study and prayer groups; family, couples, and singles groups.

All these groups may be looking for a different type of

program. If you approach them in an open way, explaining what you would like to do and trying to show them how their group's concerns relate to peace, you may be invited to one of their regular meetings.

Some program ideas.

Prepare your presentations with your audience in mind. Find a topic that might interest them, e.g., draft and conscientious objection for a youth group, nuclear war and the challenge of faith for the prayer group, the economic costs of the arms race for young couples, or whatever seems challenging and interesting for that group of people.

Present people with pertinent data to back up your arguments, but try not to overwhelm them with facts. Show why the issue is important for them and why they should become involved. Illustrate your talk with examples and refer to prominent people whom they might respect.[2] And since you are speaking to people with a religious background, refer to scriptures, to statements of religious leaders, and to resolutions from denominational bodies when appropriate.[3]

In your discussions you will often have to deal with political and economic issues but beware of becoming overly concerned about factual data and questions that deal exclusively with political arguments. Try to keep your discussion centered on what you consider to be most important, especially on the moral and spiritual values that you and your audience hold in common.

Close your presentation with suggestions for ways to change the situation you have described. Offer your audience some ways to involve themselves in study and action for peace. Have literature available for people to take and read. Have petitions for them to sign and take. Encourage then to do at least one thing to promote peace.

Invite your audience to form a study group, to join your group, or in some other way continue to explore the issues you have raised. Get the names, addresses, phone numbers, and interests of those who seem especially concerned. Make yourself available to speak to other groups and to help this group. Find ways to help them plan their own follow-up meetings or arrange ongoing programs.

Program series.

The next step might be a series of programs on a peace theme, sponsored by a congregation, by several congregations, or by a local interfaith group. A program series within a congregation might have certain advantages, especially if many members of the congregation have not yet been introduced to their denomination's stands on these issues. In some congregations, any program series on peace might first need to address the issue of how faith is related to politics. These issues may best be dealt with in a congregational group.

A particularly effective type of program series would be a month-long emphasis on a peace theme in all aspects of a congregation's life. The theme would pervade worship services, be the topic for sermons and special educational programs, find its way into the children's religion classes, and be the subject for discussion at the meetings of all the groups connected with the congregation. Every congregational group would pursue in-depth studies of the topic from their own special perspectives. The month might end with a special day of celebration. A time for study and worship on this day could include a special commitment to peacemaking by the congregation and its members. A picnic or pot-luck supper could round out the celebration.

On a smaller scale, a congregation could arrange a series of discussions on the denomination's teachings on a special issue, such as the nuclear arms race. This could be held as a special series or the topic might be the one chosen for one of the congregation's regularly scheduled series, such as the ones many churches have during Lent.

Several films and audio-visuals can make an especially attractive series. Possible themes include: nuclear war (using films such as *The War Game, War Without Winners, On the Beach,* and slide shows such as *The Last Slide Show*), war in the twentieth century (using films on World Wars I and II and Vietnam, such as *All Quiet on the Western Front*), peacemakers (including the film *Excuse Me, America!* and films on Gandhi, King and others), injustice, hunger, racism, protest movements.[4]

Many other types of program series are possible in a congregation. Some will use outside resource people while others will take advantage of the many knowledgeable people within the local community.

Congregational programs could be opened to other congregations or to the general public. You may attract some people by publishing notices of these events in local newspapers and in the bulletins of other churches and temples. (You might even want to involve persons from other congregations in these programs.)

However you do this, be sure there is some follow-up. Perhaps the congregation will make a special commitment to peace and form a peace task force or study group.

———————————SAMPLE PROGRAM SERIES———————

The Teachings of the Church on War and Peace
(A six-part series developed by the Social Action Bureau of the Diocese of Allentown)

1. "Why Must We Speak About Peace?"
   — Peacemaking in today's interconnected world.
   — Introduction to the arms race.
   — The church's response.

---

2. There are many useful quotations from military and political leaders such as President Eisenhower, General Omar Bradley, Lord Mountbatten, and George Kennan. (See: *The Defense Monitor,* Vol. IX, numbers 4 & 6 [1980] and Vol. X, number 2 [1981]; *Atlantic Monthly,* January 1981; and *Christianity and Crisis,* May 26, 1980.) See also *Quotes: Nuclear War* (Center for Defense Information. $2.)

3. See *To Proclaim Peace,* a collection of denominational statements available from FOR.

4. See Appendix for a few selected films.

2. *"Church Teachings on War and Peace"*
   — *The just war tradition.*
   — *Its application today; its weaknesses.*
   — *The nonviolent tradition.*

3. *"Economic & Social Realities of the Arms Race"*
   — *Magnitude of the arms race.*
   — *The destructive capacity of nuclear weaponry.*
   — *Film: "War Without Winners".*

4. *"The Response of Faith"*
   — *What is the true source of our security?*
   — *The Gospel of Christ's Kingdom.*
   — *Forming Christian conscience today.*
   — *Christian relations with the State.*
   — *The history of suffering love.*

5. *"Alternatives to War and Conflict"*
   — *Nature of conflict; alternatives to its resolution on individual and interpersonal levels.*
   — *Conflict resolution and alternatives to war.*
   — *What can your parish do?*

6. *"Setting Priorities"*
   — *Action planning for World Day of Peace.*
   — *Penance & Eucharist: our call to human priorities.*

Congregational Study Groups

A study group is sometimes a recognized part of a congregation; it might be responsible for providing the congregation with educational materials or action suggestions. An unofficial group will function differently and may even be an interfaith group. The needs and concerns of a particular study group and of the congregation with which it is connected will help determine the group's direction; but you might want to encourage people to integrate spiritual concerns and public witnessing into their study group.[5]

Beginning a group.

Start a study group with a few friends or interested members of your congregation. Notify others of your meetings through congregational bulletins and announcements. The day before the first meeting, a few key phone calls will remind people to come.

Begin in an up-beat manner, perhaps with a speaker or a film. Include some time for people to share their concerns and mention what they would like the study group to do. Don't let the meeting drag on interminably, but don't let it end before you have made some tentative plans on the group's future directions, including setting the time and place for the next meeting.

People may want to covenant together to meet for a certain number of weeks, even though some might want to keep the number of meetings open. The most effective arrangement might be a focussed study for a few weeks with the option of extending the study group if there is interest.

Your choice of topics and resources is important. You might want to study a certain book or use one of the study guides on the arms race now available. You might want to use speakers and audio-visuals as part of your programs. Or you might want to study an issue from several points of view, reading contrasting authors, viewing opposing films (such as *The SALT Syndrome* and *War Without Winners*), and bringing in several people to speak on a certain topic. Try to find resources that illuminate the topic you choose from various angles.

Group dynamics.

Many groups encounter the problem of how to keep people coming. It is obvious that the topic chosen must interest the group but other things must also be noticed.

Regular times and places for meetings are important. Meet once or twice a month in the congregation's meeting room or someone's home; meet after services on a specified week each month. Reminders are often helpful to members of the group. (And outsiders might be invited to join by public announcements or personal invitations.)

Groups should stick to the topic agreed upon and avoid too lengthy discussions on issues that interest only a few people. Sticking to a time limit is extremely important; meetings should end by a certain time unless all agree to stay later.

Involve as many people as possible in your meetings. Arrange for different people to facilitate meetings, to lead discussions, or to give presentations. Involve people in something they want to do and which they find interesting. Try also to help everyone feel comfortable enough so that they can disagree, ask difficult questions, and participate in discussions. Include some feedback mechanisms (such as an evaluation at the end of meetings) so those present can express their concerns about the content and dynamics of a meeting.

Be aware of the size of a group. If there are too many people, consider splitting into two or more separate groups.

Watch out particularly for stagnation. To help prevent this, have the group set goals for itself and decide on a time frame in which to accomplish them (e.g., finishing one book in three sessions), and find ways for the groups to reach out to other members of the congregations (such as planning a worship service or program) and become involved in public witnesses (supporting a petition campaign or sponsoring a weekly vigil).

---

5. World Peacemaker groups seek to combine development of the spiritual life ("the inward journey") with activities for peace ("the outward journey"). See their *Handbook for World Peacemaker Groups.* ($1.00).

Ongoing study groups might want to consider a number of issues. These may not be as focussed as a single topic study group, but they offer opportunities for congregational members to continue to educate themselves on issues. These groups should find ways to be a leaven in the congregation. They should especially beware of just sitting around and studying issues as mere intellectual exercises.

Study groups need to have some form of action flowing from their study. This may be as simple as a letter-writing campaign or placing an advertisement in a local newspaper. Or a group might plan a peace convocation or vigil. At least, they should spread their educational programs to their own congregations.

Relating to the wider community.

Some study groups may find that they lack credibility in their congregation or community. This may be due to a misrepresentation of the group or maybe even due to the group's own problems. This might be relieved if the group not only continues its peacework with special care but also involves itself in supporting activities of other groups. Co-sponsoring a hunger walk or an OXFAM Fast for a World Harvest can help build bridges. The group thus shows its positive interest in alleviating world and local problems and has another opportunity to show the links between peace concerns and meeting basic human needs.

Study groups can strengthen community and congregational efforts for peace. In Latin America, small base communities (*comunidades de base*) meet to pray, study, and act, reflecting on the message of the scripture and putting it into practice in their lives. These groups have had a major influence in the churches of Latin America.[6] Perhaps congregational peace groups can do this in the United States.[7]

Integrating Peace into Congregational Programs

Peace is not only a concern for study groups but should become an integral part of all the specific educational programs of a congregation. Peace should become part of the curriculum for Sunday schools and study groups, for confirmation classes and for instruction programs for those thinking of joining the congregation.

6. A short description of these communities, by Jim O'Callahan, entitled *Comunidades de Bases: Agents for Change in Latin America,* is available from the Catholic Peace Fellowship, 339 Lafayette St., New York, NY 10012. (15¢)
7. For more ideas on groups and process, see: Henry Fagan, *Empowerment: Skills for Parish Social Action* (Paulist Press $3.95), and Virginia Cooper, et al., *Resource Manual for a Living Revolution.* (Available from FOR: $7.50 plus 20% for handling.)

Education Programs for Youth

Children's classes are the obvious place to begin systematic peace education. Most congregations with children have established programs into which peace can be incorporated in terms of both content and the methods of instruction.

Many younger children may not be able to deal directly with peace and justice issues. But there are several programs which have developed materials to help children learn skills and attitudes which help them deal creatively with conflict.[8] These programs utilize many games and exercises that promote cooperation and nonviolence; they can be integrated into the classes for children in a local congregation. In fact, some denominational publishers have already incorporated them into their children's books and manuals.

Cooperative games can also be used during religious education classes and for special children's or intergenerational workshops and retreats.[9] These help lessen some of the unhealthy aspects of the competitive spirit that pervade so many sports programs.

Story-telling can play an important role in developing peace concerns in children. Children enjoy hearing and dramatizing stories. Read stories that emphasize peace, justice, and sharing, using resources from your religious tradition or works of fiction.[10]

Peace and justice themes can be incorporated directly into the children's educational programs. Some denominational publishers already include sections on peace, disarmament, conscientious objection, and other issues in their textbooks. Use these and supplement them with other materials developed to help teach young people in these areas.[11] Some people might design their own curriculum materials to be used for special educational

programs (such as youth retreats) or as part of the year's study.

Combine work in conflict resolution with education in issues of war and peace, especially for junior and senior high school students. (In particular, raise questions about conscientious objection and military service.)[12] Incorporate not only discussions, but also readings, audiovisuals, and various exercises to involve the whole young person in the educational process.

These educational efforts should allow for an action dimension. Encourage young people to become active promoters of justice and peace. Children of all ages can become involved in fund-raising activities for hunger concerns, such as food drives and hunger walks. Older children and teenagers might be able to help local social service groups. And many young people can become involved in specific peacemaking activities. High school students throughout the country have demonstrated, leafletted, and taken part in other protest activities. In one Vermont community, high school students distributed literature and helped educate their neighbors about the nuclear arms race before a local referendum for a nuclear weapon freeze. In December 1978, while their parents were demonstrating at the Pentagon, some children visited governmental offices and left a letter at the

---

8. The Children's Creative Response to Conflict Program (Box 271, Nyack, NY 10960) has developed a manual, *Friendly Classroom for a Small Planet* ($6.95). They also have workshops to train those who work with children. *A Manual on Children and Nonviolence* is available from Friends Peace Committee, 1515 Cherry St., Philadelphia, PA 19102 ($5.50)

9. *The New Games Book* ($6.95), and *Cooperative Sports and Games* ($5.95) are available from FOR. (Add 20% for postage)

10. See *For Children: A Booklist.* (War Resisters League, 50¢) To help children understand the reality of Hiroshima, read Eleanor Coerr's *Sadako and the Thousand Paper Cranes.* (Available from FOR. $1.25 plus 20% postage.)

11. Two books meant for helping families in these areas may be especially useful: Jacqueline Haessly, *Peacemaking: Family Activities for Justice and Peace.* (Paulist Press, $2.45; available from FOR).

Kathleen and James McGinnis, *Parenting for Peace and Justice.* (Orbis. $4.95.)

A comprehensive guide for teaching peace and justice on both elementary and secondary levels is *Educating for Peace and Justice: A Manual for Teachers* by James and Kathleen McGinnis, available from Institute for Peace and Justice.

Vol. I: National Dimensions ($9.00); Vol. II: Global Dimensions ($9.00); Vol. III: Religious Dimensions ($9.00); Vol. IV: Teacher Background Readings ($5.00). (All four volumes for $28.00).

Though largely from a Christian perspective, these books provide ideas for classes, exercises, and activities for children from all religious traditions on a variety of topics.

12. Contact FOR's Youth Action Program for Resources.

White House asking Amy Carter to talk to her father about ending the arms race.

Other educational experiences for young people might include special peace worship services, peace retreats and workshops, and visits to groups that work for justice and peace (e.g., a local Catholic Worker house). Young people can be encouraged to write essays or create posters and drawings on peace themes. Children might also be urged to hand in war toys at special services, especially before Chanukkah or Christmas.

In these and other ways, a congregation can help young people pray and reflect on war and peace, discern their responsibilities, and move toward becoming active peacemakers.

Adult Education

Education in peace should also pervade the congregation's adult education programs and the educational aspects of all the various groups in a congregation.

Some congregations have continuing religious education programs for adults. These programs or study groups might want to use a study guide on the arms race. Special continuing education programs, especially those held at certain times during the year, are also occasions for special peace programs.

Most congregations have some sort of educational program for those who are considering joining the congregation or denomination. These might include discussions to show that peace and justice are integral concerns of the life of faith.

Many congregations have small groups that meet regularly to study the scriptures. Urge them to study the peace and justice themes in scripture. With the help of biblical commentaries and of books on peace themes in the Bible, they might study such recurring themes as:

- God's vision of *shalom*: Isaiah 2:1-5; 9:1-7; 11:1-10; Micah 4:1-5; Zachariah 9:9-12; Psalm 72; Matthew 5:1-13; Luke 6:20-38; John 15:12-17; 2 Corinthians 5:1-13; Revelations 21:1-6; etc.
- The inadequacy of military power: Psalms 20:7-8; 33:16-19; 147:10-11; Isaiah 30:13-14; 31:1-4; Hosea 10:13-14; Zachariah 4:6; 2 Corinthians 10:3-5; etc.
- True and false peace: Leviticus 26; Isaiah 59; Jeremiah 6:13-14; Hosea 10:13-14; Luke 19:41-44; John 14:25-31; Ephesians 6:10-20; 1 Thessalonians 5:1-23; etc.
- Where is true security? Isaiah 31:1-9; Luke 12:13-21.

Other suggested themes for study include causes of war, suffering love, war in the Bible, and the nature of power.[13]

Some prayer groups have an educational aspect for some of their meetings. Explore with them the relation of prayer and peacemaking,[14] and invite them to begin this search as part of their continuing prayer life. At least one prayer group was so concerned that they became a World Peacemaker group, combining the work of prayer with the work of peace.[15]

Other groups might also make peace one of their concerns. A women's group might use the study guide developed by United Presbyterian Women.[16] A social justice committee might arrange special study programs on peace or sponsor a monthly issues forum after services. A hunger group might study the relation of social to military expenditures.[17] A drama group might stage plays or readings on peace themes several times a year.[18]

Approach all the groups in a congregation. Ask them to take up peacemaking as one of their priorities, something to pray over, study about, and act upon. They might then sponsor regular peace projects or annual events and provide programs and information for themselves and the congregation.

If no group does this, a study group may have to fill the gap. But hopefully the congregation and several groups will begin to see peacemaking not as an option, but as an essential dimension of their faith life.

Ongoing Peace Education

The most effective peace education in a congregation will occur when the whole congregation is continually reminded of their calling to be peacemakers.

To facilitate this, individual congregations might establish special peacemaking task forces, committees, or ministries, which would be responsible for furthering peace in that congregation. This group would reach out to congregational members, provide materials for small study groups, help develop a congregational peace resource center, foster the peacemaking activities of individuals in the congregation, and assist in training others in peace education and advocacy.

This peace group can be a significant sign of the congregation's commitment to peace. Its work will be given greater significance if a rabbi, minister, deacon, or other person is designated to work full or part-time with them. New York's West Park Presbyterian Church has one minister who devotes half of her time to peacemaking activities.

---

14. See the articles by Jim Wallis and Henri Nouwen in *Sojourners*, August 1978; March 1979; May 1979.

15. See note 6.

16. *New Communities for Peace*. (United Presbyterian Women, 1511 Interchurch Center, 475 Riverside Drive, New York, NY 10115. $2.00)

17. See Ruth Leger Sivard, *World Military & Social Expenditures*. (Annual) (Available from FOR. $4.00 plus postage)

18. See especially James Stegenga's play, "Dunbar's Bremen," (*Christianity and Crisis*, Jan. 19, 1981). Reprinted in reader's format by FOR's Covenant Peacemaking Program, $1.00 each; 10 for $9.00; 100 for $80.

---

13. See list of resources for bible study at the end of this chapter.

Even without a special peace advocate or official committee, individuals or small study groups have many opportunities to keep peace issues before a congregation.

Use bulletin board displays to spread the peace message. Place notices of events and quotes on peace in congregational newsletters and bulletins. Regular announcements of peace issues and educational events may encourage people to participate in various peacemaking activities.

You might want to set up a literature table in the rear of the church or temple and at congregational events. Have a literature table with "Pentagon cookies" at a church bazaar. (People pay for a whole cookie but only get half.)

Ask the congregational librarian to include a few peace books and magazines in a special peace section.

You might also try to persuade the congregation to set up an annual peace day.[19] There is perhaps no better way to help people see the importance of peace than by making it a part of their lives and establishing peace traditions in a congregation.

Interfaith Peace Efforts

While the congregation is perhaps the most crucial place for peacemaking work, interfaith efforts nourish and sustain these activities.

There are many possible types of interfaith peace groups. In some places, including Vermont, Northern California, and Wisconsin, a committee of the regional ecumenical agency has sought to foster peace work. In Los Angeles, a Jewish and Episcopalian congregation joined together to form the Interfaith Center to Reverse the Arms Race. In Louisville, Kentucky, several persons formed a Council on Religion and Peacemaking which has gained the support of several denominational leaders. In other places, people from many religious groups have formed their own independent interfaith groups. And, in some areas, individuals have promoted interfaith efforts nearly single-handedly.

Interfaith Convocations

Interfaith work can start with even a small group of people. They might begin by planning an event, such as a Peace Sabbath celebration, as a way to bring interested people together, to stir up interest in the area, and perhaps to form a larger local peace group. People in hundreds of communities have held conferences, seminars, and convocations as part of interfaith Peace Sabbath celebrations; in some places, these have become an annual tradition.

A major program is a difficult task. But a small group of people can initiate the planning for such an event. The secret of success, though, is to involve as many people as possible from different groups in your community. Contact rabbis, other clergy, ecumenical and denominational executives, as well as people involved in congregational and denominational peace and justice work. Seek input from local groups which might be sympathetic, such as United Nations Association, League of Women Voters, Gray Panthers, Church Women United, Council of Jewish Women, a community center, or a social change group. It can be especially helpful to contact local colleges, especially their campus ministry or chaplain's offices. A college might help co-sponsor the event, provide facilities, and even arrange for special speakers to complement your program.

The representatives of all these groups should be invited to sponsor and share in planning the event. Some might be asked to speak or to lead worship services, workshops, and Bible study groups. All should be asked to help publicize the event especially to the members of their own groups.

Use volunteers from as many groups as possible to help contact speakers, prepare the facilities, staff registration tables, and in other ways help the event function smoothly.

At the event itself, set up an area for local and national groups to display literature and sell materials. Contact national groups and ask them to send information on various issues and strategies for peacemaking.

And find ways to follow up after the meeting. Your registration form might include a place for people to indicate their interest in continuing involvement through a study group, a legislative action network, a direct action group or in some other way. Contact these people afterwards with a letter, a phone call, or by sending them a copy of your newsletter. Connect them with other people who are involved in peace activities in the community.

---

19. Check with the FOR each year for suggested dates for Peace Sabbath. New Peace Sabbath packets are prepared each year for congregational use.

Other Possible Efforts

A local interfaith peace committee might not want to begin with a major conference. Instead, it might help prepare and distribute materials to different congregations, assist them in planning their own programs, and facilitate other efforts. It might also help arrange itineraries for major speakers in the area, seeing that they get to various congregations or community groups.

Some groups will want to meet regularly for study and to plan public witnesses for peace. They might profitably combine weekly or monthly study groups with occasional public activities or conferences. Subcommittees might be set up to work on different issues; certain persons could be designated to be responsible for specific issues and projects.

A committee might also sponsor a weekly vigil for peace or occasional public witnesses or demonstrations. Advertisements in a local newspaper, press releases, and public statements on issues help educate the public on these issues and even attract new members.

If desired, a peace committee could sponsor annual events for peace. Possibilities include Memorial Day picnics for peace, interfaith services on Martin Luther King's birthday (January 15), Peace Sabbath celebrations, and vigils and fasts for the anniversaries of the bombings of Hiroshima and Nagasaki (August 6 and 9).

Other projects might include: getting peace education or alternatives to violence programs into local schools and congregations; training speakers and teams to visit community groups, service clubs, and congregations; establishing local speakers' bureaus; setting up displays and literature tables at public events and helping denominational groups set up displays at their meetings; arranging special peace study days for clergy, religious educators, and others.

An office, perhaps in a local church or synagogue, could provide a center for meetings and become a resource center with a library of books, brochures, and audio-visuals.

If funding is available, an interfaith peace group might hire a full-time or part-time staff person for one year or a longer period. This person could speak at functions of local congregations, visit local pastors and rabbis, hold workshops and training sessions, and, in general, be a resource person for the community and for local churches and temples.

Interfaith peace groups provide support for the efforts of local congregations, inspire other congregations to become involved, and encourage people from different denominations to work together for peace. These interfaith groups can thus express the unity of religious response which is needed today.

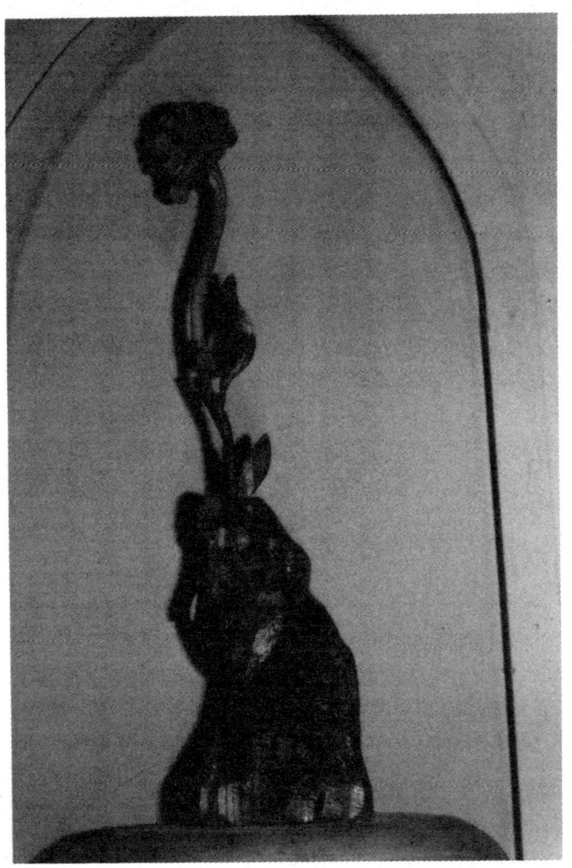

"The Hand and the Rose," by Stuart Groshong. Donated to FOR office in Nyack, this statue was carved out of charred wood from a church destroyed by atomic blast in Hiroshima.

Resources

Study Guides

Christopher Grannis, Arthur Laffin, & Elin Schade, *The Risk of the Cross: Christian Discipleship in the Nuclear Age.* (Seabury. $5.95) *

George Hunsinger, ed., *The Riverside Church Disarmament Reader: A Model Course for Disarmament Studies.* (Riverside Church Disarmament Program. $15)

Mary Lou Kownacki, ed., *A Race to Nowhere: An Arms Race Primer for Catholics.* (Pax Christi USA. $3)

Donald B. Kraybill, *Facing Nuclear War.* (Herald Press. $8.95)

Charlie Lord, *The Rule of the Sword: A Study Guide on Technological Militarism.* (Faith and Life Press. $1)

William Osterle and John Donaghy, ed., *Peace Theology and the Arms Race: Readings on Arms and Disarmament.* (College Theology Society Publications, St. Joseph University, Philadelphia, PA 19131. $7)

William W. Rankin, *Countdown to Disaster: A Study in Christian Ethics.* (Forward Movement Publications. $2.95)

Maynard Shelley, *New Call for Peacemakers: A New Call to Peacemaking Study Guide.* (Faith and Life Press. $2)

Sojourners, *A Matter of Faith: The Church and the Nuclear Arms Race.* (Sojourners. $3.50)

---

*Available from FOR; please add 20% for postage and handling.

Jim Wallis, ed., *Waging Peace: A Handbook for the Struggle Against Nuclear Weapons.* (Harper & Row. $4.95)

Bible Study Aids

Dale Aukerman, *Darkening Valley: A Biblical Perspective on Nuclear War.* (Seabury. $8.95)

Richard Cassidy, *Jesus, Politics and Society: A Study of Luke's Gospel.* (Orbis. $7.95)

Vernard Eller, *War and Politics from Genesis to Revelation.* (Herald Press. $8.95)

John Ferguson, *The Politics of Love: The New Testament and Nonviolent Revolution.* (Fellowship. $3) *

John Ferguson, *War and Peace in the World's Religions.* (Oxford. $3.95) *

Christopher Grannis & others, *The Risk of the Cross.* (Seabury. $5.95) *

Abraham Joshua Heschel, *The Prophets.* (2 volumes) (Harper. $4.95 each volume)

Jean Lassere, *War and the Gospel.* (Herald Press. $6.95)

Millard C. Lind, *Yahweh Is a Warrior.* (Herald Press.)

Richard McSorley, S.J., *New Testament Basis of Pacifism.* (Center for Peace Studies, Georgetown University, 2 O'Gara Hall, Washington, DC 20057. $2.25) *

Ronald Sider, *Christ and Violence.* (Herald Press. $4.95) *Cry Justice! The Bible on Hunger and Poverty.* (Paulist. $2.95) *Rich Christians in an Age of Hunger.* (Paulist. $4.95)

Allan Solomonow, ed., *Roots of Jewish Nonviolence.* (Jewish Peace Fellowship. $2) *

William Stringfellow, *Conscience and Obedience: Romans 13 and Revelation 13.* (Word. $3.25)

Andre Trocme, *Jesus and Nonviolent Revolution.* (Herald Press. $7.95) *

Jim Wallis, *The Call to Conversion: Recovering the Gospel for These Times.* (Harper & Row. $6.95)

John Howard Yoder, *The Politics of Jesus.* (Eerdmans. $4.95) *

Also refer to bible commentaries and other books, including those published by Herald Press, Orbis Books, and Paulist Press.

Books about Peacemakers

Philip Hallie, *Lest Innocent Blood Be Shed: The Story of The Village of Le Chambon and How Goodness Happened There.* (Harper. $4.95) *

Marjorie Hope and James Young, *The Struggle for Humanity: Agents of Change in a Violent World.* (Orbis Books. $6.95) *

Allan Hunter, *Courage in Both Hands.* (Ballantine. $1.50) *

Also see biographies of such peacemakers as Dorothy Day, A.J. Muste, Martin Luther King, Jr., M. K. Gandhi, Dom Helder Camara, and Thomas Merton as well as articles on peacemakers in publications such as Fellowship.

Peace Education Groups

COPRED (Consortium on Peace Research, Education, and Development), Center for Peaceful Change, Kent State University, Kent OH 44242.

Global Education Associates, 552 Park Avenue, East Orange, NJ 07017.

Institute for Justice and Peace, 4144 Lindell Blvd., #400, St. Louis, MO 63108.

Institute for World Order, 777 United Nations Plaza, New York, NY 10017.

4. Activities for Peace

As you come to know the seriousness of our situation — the war, the racism, the poverty in the world — you come to realize it is not going to be changed just by words or demonstrations. It's a question of risking your life. It's a question of living your life in dramatically different ways.

Dorothy Day

Peace education should result in action for peace. The apostle James urged his readers to be "doers of the word and not hearers only deceiving yourselves." (1:22) Today the "paralysis of analysis" is still a temptation for many educational programs and study groups. But if study is oriented toward action, people find ways to use their information, to act upon their convictions, and to allay the feeling of powerlessness that often comes with the study of issues such as the arms race.

Action for peace is a special responsibility of people of faith. Jesus called the "*makers* of peace" blessed. (Matt. 5:9) And the Midrash to Numbers 19:27 notes:

It is written 'Seek peace and pursue it' (Psalm 34:15). The Law does not order you to run after or pursue the commandments, but only to fulfill them, when the appropriate time comes; that is, when *this* happens then you must do *that*. When the occasion comes for the commandments, then you are enjoined to fulfill them. But peace you must seek in your own place and run after it in another.

Peacemaking and the "ministry of reconciliation" (2 Corinthians 5:18) are truly signs of faithfulness.

Promoting peace is also a civic responsibility. Insofar as people have a share in government, they are responsible for the actions of public authorities. Responsible citizenship means promotion of peace and justice in the public realm. As the 1971 Synod of Catholic Bishops wrote in *Justice in the World*:

Action on behalf of justice and participation in the transformation of the world fully appear to us as a constitutive dimension of the preaching of the Gospel, or, in other words, of the Church's mission for the redemption of the human race and its liberation from every oppressive situation.

So it is that the peacemaking activities of congregations, congregational groups, and individual people of faith are manifestations of the peacemaking work of God in the world. The activities of these groups also have political significance since this involvement adds legitimacy to peace efforts and may encourage other people of faith to become involved.

Many types of activities are possible. While some might be done within a congregation or denomination, others

might take the form of witnesses to other religious groups or to the community at large. Other activities are meant to influence governmental officials directly at the town, state, or national level.

Actions should be chosen carefully and carried out after serious planning. Prayerful personal and community preparation can make the difference between an action that is merely another demonstration and one that is a witness flowing from faith.

Before beginning any activity, assess the issue you plan to focus on, especially in regard to how your actions can clarify the issue and encourage public support. The focus should be both short and long term. For example, if you work for a bilateral nuclear weapon freeze, recognize the ultimate goal of the abolition of nuclear weapons.

Think carefully also about the immediate and long-range goals of your actions. While ultimate goals should be set high, an immediate goal must be something more easily realizable. If your ultimate goal is to close a nearby nuclear weapons plant, an immediate goal might be 5,000 signatures of local citizens, followed by support from local and state governmental authorities. Setting immediate goals too high can lead to frustration early in a campaign. The realization of certain short-range goals can provide a sense of accomplishment, thus encouraging participants to continue the long struggle for peace.

When choosing a specific activity, it might also be helpful to ask yourself if you are hoping by this action to educate and influence others on an issue or if you are primarily interested in changing the minds or policies of political leaders. Or do you want to combine these? Different purposes demand different types of activities.

Furthermore, keep in mind that there are many different kinds of people interested in peacemaking. Some feel very uncomfortable picketing while they might be the most faithful letter-writers. Others might find it difficult to write letters but are willing to risk arrest by acts of non-violent civil disobedience. The diversity of gifts and concerns demands that there be a similar diversity of activities for peace. No one should be excluded because of an unwillingness to be involved in a certain action. Find ways to involve all interested persons and to help people support each other in their varied activities for peace.

Finally, act in a spirit of faith and hope. Immediate results may not be forthcoming, but that shouldn't deter you. Peacemaking has been compared to gardening — a slow process demanding constant, persistent, and patient care.

Following are some activities which congregations and individuals can do.

Congregational Activities

Since peacemaking is first of all a personal commitment, the congregation can be the community which urges and supports people to become active peacemakers.

This might start by making resources available for personal commitment. People might be urged to sign the World Peace Pledge.[1] Distribute the pledge during a service or print it in the weekly bulletin; collect it during a service and offer it as a sign of the commitment of people in the congregation. Or a scroll might be placed in a prominent place for signing and left there until it is sent to the FOR.

Petitions and other pledges might also be made available and collected during worship services or left in the rear of the building for people to sign at their leisure.

In some congregations, people might be urged to make covenants. These can be personal covenants, covenants of groups within the congregation, or a covenant made by the entire congregation. After the United Presbyterians' 1980 General Assembly, the United Presbyterian Peace Fellowship and the Witherspoon Society circulated a covenant which offered people various options for continuing the peacemaking efforts begun at the meeting.[2] The New Abolitionist Covenant, featured in Chapter 6, grew out of several prayerful meetings of people from the Fellowship of Reconciliation, New Call to Peacemaking, Pax Christi USA, Sojourners, and World Peacemakers. Small groups might adopt a covenant and then bring it to their congregations. The congregation might itself adopt a covenant as its plan of action or provide support for those who have adopted a

covenant, acknowledging and affirming these covenants. This might take place in the context of a service.

Groups of people in a congregation might also recommend the consideration of certain resolutions by the various groups in the congregation or at the church's annual meeting. The congregation could then consider and vote on that issue and, if it passes, urge other denominational bodies to consider it.

Congregations, committees, pastors, rabbis, and individuals might also prepare and distribute pastoral letters urging other people of faith to examine issues and take stands.

To help further peace work in the local congregation and nationally, a congregation might designate a certain day each year for a special peacemaking offering. At their 1980 General Assembly, the United Presbyterian Church USA requested each congregation to have an annual offering to support peacemaking initiatives and educational efforts throughout the church. Twenty-five percent of the offering is designated for the peace activities of the local church, twenty-five percent for the activities of regional bodies, and the rest to help support the national efforts of the denomination.

There are some other peacemaking activities which a congregation might undertake, including sponsoring refugee families. These people are often the victims of violence and oppression in their homelands.

The nuclear arms race has generated its own victims. These include not only the people of Nagasaki and Hiroshima and the native people in Micronesia, whose islands were used by the US for testing in the 1940s and 1950s. There are also those who lived near the test sites in Nevada and Utah and the soldiers who were compelled to participate in exercises during the atomic tests in those areas. A congregation might provide some support for them, establishing a special relationship with them and providing some financial, legal, and moral assistance.[3] Other forms of support for victims of war and militarism include: aid for medical services in war-torn areas, food relief for others (even those on the "other side"), and special aid for children left homeless by war.

In any congregation, there are many young people who also need help and support as they consider questions of military service, selective service registration, and the draft. They need help in forming their conscience on these issues, in seeing alternatives to militarism, and in making decisions which might put them in social or legal jeopardy. A congregation might set up study groups or workshops for young people which would present the issues in the light of religious faith. The young people might want to follow this up with their own rap groups. It would also be helpful if a congregation saw that there are a few people trained as draft counselors or that outside draft counselors are invited in regularly. The church or temple might also set up its own registry for any conscien-

---

1. Pledge brochures, buttons and posters are available from FOR's Covenant Peacemaking Program. Brochures are 10¢ each; 100 or more; plus 20% handling. A presentation of the pledges will be made each year to officials at the White House and the United Nations.

2. The Covenant's options included praying for peace, establishing peace task forces in local churches or presbyteries, and seeking financial support for church peacemaking efforts.

3. Contact: National Committee for Radiation Victims, 317 Pennsylvania Ave. SE, Washington, DC 20003.

tious objectors to supplement the national registries set up by some denominations.

Some young people may make decisions on these issues which will involve them in serious legal and social jeopardy. Conscientious objectors may face societal pressures of various kinds and may be unable to obtain c.o. status from a draft board. A congregation should support these young people, providing letters of support and helping to pay costs incurred by prosecution. Some young people might decide in good conscience that they are unable to register for a draft or to accept induction. The lengthy prosecutions which might ensue are costly and potentially draining emotionally and spiritually. Local congregations should stand by these people, offering moral and financial help, even if there are some who cannot support the stand. Those who are imprisoned will need a great deal of moral and spiritual support. Studies have shown that those draft resisters during the Vietnam War who had outside support fared best in prison. Visiting those imprisoned for the sake of conscience is a pastoral responsibility of all people of faith.

Many today are beginning to question whether they should pay taxes for war. A congregation should help these people prayerfully to consider all the issues involved — not only the direct moral and legal problems but also questions of life style. It might distribute literature, arrange workshops, and form study groups on tax resistance. A congregation can also help those who conscientiously refuse to pay taxes for war by providing ways for them to live below a taxable income, assisting in case of IRS liens or seizures of money or property, sharing any court costs incurred, filing *amicus* briefs or testifying in court cases, and providing moral support. Perhaps a congregation, a religious leader, or others might follow the example of Archbishop Raymond Hunthausen of Seattle and urge tax resistance:

> Our paralyzed political process needs the catalyst of nonviolent action based on faith. We have to refuse to give incense — in our day tax dollars — to the nuclear idol. On April 15, we can vote for unilateral disarmament with our lives. Form 1040 is the place where the Pentagon enters all of our lives and asks our unthinking cooperation in the idol of nuclear destruction.

Many congregations may want to provide vocational counselling for those who are employed in weapons industries. Engineers and others may need help in finding constructive uses for their training and skills. Others may need assistance finding more secure employment than with military industries, which are at the mercy of a "boom and bust" cycle. Those who in conscience find they can no longer assist in manufacturing weapons often need special support and assistance.[4]

---

4. In early 1982, Archbishop Hunthausen announced that he was refusing half of his income taxes. Also in 1982, Bishop Leroy Matthiesen of Amarillo, Texas, set up a Solidarity Peace Fund (Diocesan Pastoral Center, Box 5644, Amarillo, TX 79107) in order to provide assistance to workers who might quit their jobs at the nearby Pantex nuclear weapons plant for reasons of conscience.

Resources and organizations who are involved in these and other issues of conscience and war are listed at the end of the chapter.

The Congregation As Witness

To Other Faith Communities:

A congregation or congregational group might reach out to other congregations in their area. They can offer to present programs to other congregations or lead study groups. They can involve these congregations in co-sponsoring events such as peace fairs, convocations, or special interfaith services.

Individuals might be designated to personally contact other religious leaders in their area on a personal basis. Set up appointments to visit local clergy in their offices and offer them assistance in beginning peace efforts in their congregations. Have someone speak at one of the regular meetings of the local ministerial association or clergy group. This is an important forum in which you can meet clergy from many denominations and involve them in serious discussions on the issue. This might result in the formation of a local study group of clergy and others or in an invitation for a speaker at one of their churches or synagogues. Someone speaking on peace at a clergy meeting might be what is needed to move a few clergy to actually do something for peace in their congregations.

A congregational group might pass out leaflets at public religious events or after services at different congregations each week. They might even leaflet religious rallies, as Baltimore CALC and the Brethren Peace Fellowship did at a June 1981 Billy Graham Crusade.

A group might also arrange to set up tables and displays at revivals and rallies, at religious events, and at the meetings of groups such as Church Women United.

Demonstrations and forms of street theatre or tableaus are also effective when held outside a building where a religious event is taking place. During the 1976 Eucharistic Congress in Philadelphia, several groups staged tableaus on issues such as governmental support of torture; on August 6, many vigiled outside a Mass for the military and then held an alternative peace liturgy.

Within One's Own Denomination:

Congregations can also work for peace with national and regional bodies of their own denominations.

Many denominations have national and regional bodies which deal with peace issues. Find out what resources are available and what programs they are planning. Offer suggestions for possible projects and available resources. This is particularly important on a regional level where a board might be persuaded to do more for peace if pressured. Urge the board to send literature to local congregations, provide support for a regional peace task force or special peace ministry, or present resolutions or recommendations to denominational boards or annual meetings. In turn, these boards need moral and financial assistance from people in local congregations.

Congregational groups can present programs at the annual regional or occasional national meetings of their denomination. They can help the missions or social concerns board prepare displays and literature tables. Individuals might lead workshops on issues or set up special study or prayer groups during the meeting. A congregation or other group might sponsor a special peacemaking breakfast during the meeting.[5]

A congregation or group might also bring resolutions to the floor of these meetings. While resolutions from individuals and various boards may find support at these meetings, more weight is often attached to resolutions which have the support of local congregations.

Local congregations might also offer suggestions to national and regional denominational bodies for their consideration.

Congregational Public Witness

Public Worship.

Since the congregation is first of all a worshipping community of faith, it can begin to express its public witness in worship.

During the Vietnam war, worship played a central part in some protest activities. Quakers sponsored weekly silent vigils against the war on town greens and held meetings for worship outside the White House. Several times Catholic or Episcopal clergy were arrested when

they sought to celebrate the Eucharist in the Pentagon. Many churches held special services or vigils in which they offered draft resisters symbolic "sanctuary" in their buildings.

In 1980 and 1981, interfaith worship services were held outside the Washington, D.C., hotels where the Arms Bazaars were held.[6] In 1981, Jews held public observances of Tisha B'Av on August 9 at the White House and the Soviet Embassy in Washington, and throughout the country, in protest of the nuclear arms race.[7] Other groups have held worship services at nuclear weapons facilities, at the offices of defense contractors, at universities and military research facilities, and at federal offices.

Congregations and other groups might sponsor silent vigils, interfaith services and other forms of worship at appropriate times and places. These might include public fasting, held in a house of worship or even at a military facility. Those involved might also wear ashes or sackcloth or use other signs of repentance and resistance.

Churches might be requested to toll their bells and hold periods of silent reflection at special times, especially in commemoration of the bombings of Hiroshima (August 6: 8:15 A.M.) and Nagasaki (August 9: 11:02 A.M.).

Processions and pilgrimages have been used as protests, with people walking to military facilities, to congressional offices, to denominational offices, and even to traditional pilgrimage sites, bearing religious symbols and protest signs. For example, in spring 1981, the British FOR sponsored a 900-mile pilgrimage for peace which started at the Abbey of Iona (a medieval pilgrimage site and now a center of church renewal, off the coast of Scotland) and ended at Canterbury Cathedral, another ancient pilgrimage site and now the spiritual center of the Anglican communion. On the way they often stopped at military bases and at those places where nuclear weapons are stored in Great Britain.

Symbolic actions connected with worship have also been utilized. During Holy Week in 1977, several groups held torture tableaus at selected sites in Washington in opposition to U.S. support of regimes which practice torture. On April 25, 1981, several FOR groups in

---

5. For several years, both the United Presbyterian and the Southern Presbyterian Peace Fellowships have held breakfasts at their respective General Assemblies. At these, they have had a major speaker and also presented awards to persons who have distinguished themselves in their work for peace.

6. Contact Sojourners Peace Ministry for details.

7. Contact New Jewish Agenda for details.

Indiana held a noisy "march around the walls of Jericho" at Grissom Air Force Base. Religious symbols, such as crosses and Stars of David, have been erected outside the perimeters of military bases. In South Vietnam during the war, Buddhists erected altars in the streets.

Some people have been arrested for public prayer at nuclear weapons facilities, especially at the Amarillo, Texas, Pantex plant and the Bangor, Washington, Trident base. At the latter, Jim Douglass risked his life and was imprisoned as he sought to pray at the missile silos.[8]

These are only a few ways to worship publicly as a witness for peace.

Public Actions.

Congregational groups might also support local and national demonstrations and meetings. A congregation might join a march carrying a banner identifying themselves and encourage other congregations to form a special religious contingent in a march. Or they might join with other religious groups to sponsor a special religious action. During the 1978 United Nations Special Session on Disarmament, a religious observance was held, featuring workshops, a worship service, and a march to the U.N. Religious groups, notably Sojourners and the Episcopal Peace Fellowship, have been among the main organizers from both the religious and peace community for the demonstrations at the Arms Bazaars in Washington.

Congregations can also have a special presence at local events. Set up a literature table and display at a town fair or at the meetings or conventions of groups such as educational associations. Put a peace float in a parade, as a Vermont church young adult group did in a July 4th parade in 1980. March in the Memorial Day parade or hold a special peace vigil during that event.

A congregation might also place peace advertisements in local newspapers, especially before holy days or important elections. The ad might be a simple statement signed by clergy and laity with endorsements by various groups.

Congregations should advertise special programs or worship services. For example, for the past two years several United Presbyterian churches in New York City have placed an ad in the religious events calendar of the newspaper announcing special Peace Sabbath services.

The range of actions a congregation or congregational groups can take is limited only by the willingness of people to act and their creativity in witnessing for peace.

Corporate Responsibility.

The concept of stewardship of resources is central to the life and thought of many churches and temples.

Congregations might first of all examine the banks and lending institutions they use. Do these institutions engage in discriminatory practices against the poor, against

racial minorities or women? Do they practice red-lining? Are they closely allied to military contractors? If so, a congregation might try to influence these banks to change their practices or, if that is not possible, withdraw all their funds.[9]

Congregations, denominational bodies, and other religious institutions should also examine their investment portfolios. Are they profiting by investment in military contractors or in firms which practice discrimination or make unsafe or immoral products? If so, the groups might attempt to change these policies by supporting or introducing resolutions at stockholder meetings. (The Interfaith Center on Corporate Responsibility can provide assistance in this.) If this proves ineffective, they might consider investing elsewhere.[10]

Influencing Public Policy.

Peacemaking also includes working in the political arena, seeking to change local and national policies which are inimical to justice and peace. But because of their tax-exempt status, religious groups have certain limitations on the type and amount of work they can do in this area.

At the very least, encourage congregational members to become involved personally in many different types of political activities. Make available background papers on

---

8. See Douglass' article, "Saying Yes to Life," (March/April 1980 *Fellowship*.)

9. For information on specific campaigns, especially on stopping bank loans to South Africa, contact the Interfaith Center on Corporate Responsibility.

10. For information on a socially conscious mutual fund, contact: Pax World Fund, Inc., 224 State St., Portsmouth, NH 03801.

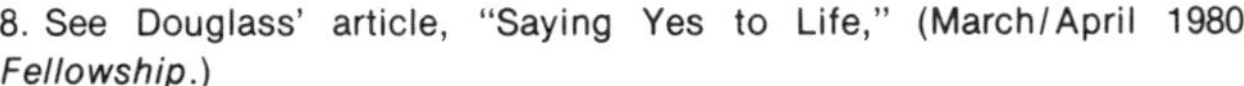

legislation which emphasize the moral and theological dimensions of issues. Circulate petitions; encourage letter-writing to legislators. On a particularly urgent issue, a congregation might send a delegation to their legislators or ask them to come to the temple or church for an evening's discussion. Some people might also seek to testify to local, state, and national committees on certain issues.

On particularly important issues, a congregation might sponsor discussions, distribute position papers, and even take public stands. Individual clergy and lay people can, of course, also indicate their positions.

Many people consider it essential to supplement grass roots peace work with involvement in national legislative work. Most denominational bodies have offices in Washington which monitor legislation, testify before congress, and even do some lobbying. These offices can provide local congregations with background information on the issues before the U.S. Congress. There are also several groups, some closely connected with religious bodies, which provide background reports and issue legislative action alerts. A congregation might subscribe to some of their publications.[11]

A congregation can become involved in legislative work at other levels. It might designate a special person or committee responsible to keep an eye on legislation, to seek out those members of the congregation who are concerned about specific issues, and to send them regular legislative alerts. It could also set up a telephone tree for emergency actions on legislation.

A whole congregation can be involved in influencing public policy. Not only can it vote resolutions on issues and refer them to governmental authorities, it can sponsor "offerings of letters," a tactic used effectively by Bread for the World groups. People are given background information and materials for writing letters. After time is allotted for writing, the letters are collected during a service as a special offering of concern.

Contact the groups working on national legislation for further ideas for action as well as for information on specific issues.

Other Congregational Activities.

Since peace and justice groups need places for their meetings and functions, a congregation can help greatly by making its facilities available for nothing or a minimal price.

A congregation can also help by referring people to those groups, letting people know of the activities and nature of the various national and local peace groups. Announcements of special programs or demonstrations could appear in congregational bulletins. The bulletin also could feature monthly reports on the nature of different peace or justice groups.

A congregation might invite people from various groups for programs, special lectures, or even for sermons. These groups might also set up literature tables and displays in the congregational buildings on a specific day; or a day might be set aside when all the groups would be invited to come.

In these ways, the congregation can serve as a center for networking and encouraging peacemaking activities.

Witness from Denominational Bodies

Denominational bodies on regional and national levels can do much to promote peace. Special boards, such as Offices of Social Action or of Church and Society can prepare and distribute materials for study and action by local congregations. Denominational offices can issue statements, release pastoral letters, support petitions, and in other ways help educate people. National assemblies can pass resolutions and direct national offices to spend time and money on programs for the entire denomination.

Regional and national offices might consider hiring staff to deal specifically with peace concerns. At least, they can direct certain boards to devote some time to these issues. A staff person on a regional level might provide educational materials, spend time visiting local congregations, provide training for people in peace work in local congregations, and help educate clergy and lay people. On a national level, staff persons can develop resources for worship, study and action, and network people in local congregations and regional bodies with other concerned peace people and organizations. They can also share the experiences of people in various congregations as they seek to promote peacemaking at the local level.[12] They might also be involved in national peace efforts, testifying before congressional committees, providing background on legislation to denominational bodies and individual churches, and maybe even doing some lobbying. Both regional and national offices can find ways to help congregations relate to national and international peacemaking efforts, as well as to various other legislative issues.

These offices can also sponsor leadership training conferences, convocations, study days, etc. A regional denominational body might be persuaded to devote its clergy education convocation to peace issues and in other ways provide continuing peace education opportunities for people in their denomination.

---

11. IMPACT, for example, provides background on legislation and details on legislative timing, including information on when and where to write. (There is even a special Jewish section called Chai IMPACT.) For the addresses of IMPACT and other similar groups, see the end of this chapter.

12. The United Presbyterian Peacemaking Project has prepared a book sharing the experiences of several congregations in peacemaking. Entitled *Peacemaking is Under Way*, it is available from Presbyterian Distribution Service, Room 935, 475 Riverside Drive, New York, NY 10115. ($1.00)

Regional and national meetings offer many opportunities for speaking out and acting for peace. Displays with peace literature, tables with sample petitions and pledges, and peace posters provide valuable information and ideas for people to take back to their local congregations. Special peace breakfasts, peace discussion groups, and prayer groups offer opportunities for those interested to come together and share. Ideally, the major assembly speaker might consider a peace issue.

Denominational assemblies have also been occasions for special peace witnesses. During the 1980 United Methodist Church's General Conference, a delegation was commissioned to visit the White House and urge the President to seek reconciliation with Iran to avoid the use of military force. (Sadly, the meeting was held the day before the abortive rescue mission.) At the 1980 General Assembly of the Unitarian Universalist Association, 300 delegates held an early morning vigil at the nearby Kirkland Air Force Base in Albuquerque.

Many religious leaders have also taken part in public protests. For example, on April 25, 1981, the Episcopal bishop, a Catholic auxiliary bishop, and other religious leaders led a march in Denver protesting the continued manufacture of parts for nuclear weapons at the nearby Rocky Flats Weapons Plant.

In these and other ways, national and regional religious leaders and bodies witness the concern of the religious community for peace.

Dorothy Day holding prison gown signed by her cell mates.

Witness of Individuals

Of course there are times and places where congregations are not concerned about peace and may even be somewhat antipathetic to peace concerns. Here the burden of action might fall on one or a few people. But the potential for influencing others by even one person should not be overlooked. Following are a few suggestions for activities which individuals might consider:

- Pray daily for peace.

- Sign and distribute pledges and petitions.

- Leaflet churches, federal buildings, or other places.

- Enclose peace literature with letters.

- Set up displays at religious events, local fairs, etc.

- Give peace books to local city, school, and congregational libraries.

- Give people or libraries a gift subscription to a peace periodical, e.g., *Fellowship*.

- Personal witness to clergy, public officials, and others by letters, visits, or vigils.

- Personal witness to members of local churches and temples and others in the community.

- Become a key contact for legislative alert networks and spread the word on legislation to people in your area.

- Become a key contact with a national organization and spread their literature in your area.

- Become a member of the Fellowship of Reconciliation and other national peace/justice groups.

- Help bring speakers into your area.

- Participate in demonstrations or vigils in your town or elsewhere.

- Organize small support demonstrations in your town at the time of major national demonstrations.

- Get a few people together for regular vigils or for small demonstrations on appropriate occasions, e.g., April 15.

- Hold a one-person demonstration.

- Become informed on the issues and help organize meetings on issues, perhaps in other people's homes.

- Contact local FOR members for support and for possible formation of a local FOR chapter.

- Support the efforts of local and regional peace groups.

- Become involved in local draft counseling efforts.

- Consider non-payment of taxes for war.

- Find ways to nurture peace in your own life and in the lives of others.

- Volunteer some time each week with local peace and justice groups.

- Write letters to newspaper editors and legislators.

- Write an op-ed piece for local newspapers.

- Wear a peace button.

Resources

Disarmament

Nuclear War Prevention Kit (Center for Defense Information. $1)

Organizing Manual for Congregations (Interfaith Center to Reverse the Arms Race. $5 plus 20% postage.)

Draft Issues

A.J. Muste, *Of Holy Disobedience.* (Pendle Hill, $1.25) *; Robert Seeley, *Handbook for Conscientious Objectors* (CCCO. $3) *; Henry David Thoreau, *On the Duty of Civil Disobedience* (FOR. $1.50) *; *Words of Conscience: Religious Statements of Conscientious Objection* (NISBCO. $2) *

Organizations:
FOR Youth Action Program, Box 271, Nyack, NY 10960
CCCO, 2208 South Street, Philadelphia, PA 19146
NISBCO, 550 Washington Building, 15th and New York Avenue NW, Washington, DC 20005
Pax Christi Center for Conscience and War, Box 726, 5 Bigelow Rd., Cambridge, MA 02139.

Tax Resistance

God and Caesar (newsletter), CHM, Box 347, Newton, KS 67114

Handbook on the Nonpayment of War Taxes (Peacemakers. $1.50)

War Tax Packet (FOR, $1) *

William Durland, *People Pay for Peace* (Center on Law and Pacifism, $4) *

War Resisters League, *Guide to War Tax Resistance* (WRL, $6) *

Organizations:
Center on Law and Pacifism, P.O. Box 1584, Colorado Springs, CO 80901
Conscience and Military Tax Campaign, 44 Bellhaven Road, Bellport, NY 11713
National Council for A World Peace Tax Fund, 2111 Florida Avenue NW, Washington, DC 20008
Peacemakers, P.O. Box 627, Garberville, CA 95440

Corporate Responsibility

Eleanor Craig, S.L., *A Shareowner's Manual: For Church Committees for Social Responsibility in Investments.* (ICCR. $3.50 plus postage)

Interfaith Center for Corporate Responsibility (ICCR), 475 Riverside Drive, Room 566, New York, NY 10115.

Legislative Work

Register Citizen Opinion, Board of Church and Society, 100 Maryland Ave. NE, Washington, DC 20002 (35¢)

Organizations:
Bread for the World, 32 Union Square E., NY, NY 10003.
Coalition for a New Foreign and Military Policy, 120 Maryland Ave. NE, Washington, DC 20002.
Friends Committee for National Legislation, 245 Second St. NE, Washington, DC 20002.
Impact, 100 Maryland Ave. NE, Washington, DC 20002.
Network, 806 Rhode Island Ave. NE, Washington, DC 20018.

Other

Steve Brooks, et al., *A Guide to Political Fasting.* (Non-violent Tactics, 454 Willamette St., Eugene, OR 97401. $2)

Virginia Cooper et al., *Resource Manual for a Living Revolution.* (New Society Press. $5)*

William Durland, ed., *Conscience and the Law.* (Center for Law and Pacifism. $5)

Richard K. Taylor, *Blockade: A Guide to Nonviolent Intervention.* (Orbis)

Nonviolent Direct Action. (FOR. 10¢)

War Resisters League Organizer's Manual (WRL, $6) plus $1 postage)

---

*Available from FOR; please add 20% for handling.

5. The Nuclear Weapon Freeze Campaign

To improve national and international security, the United States and the Soviet Union should stop the nuclear arms race. Specifically, they should adopt a mutual freeze on the testing, production, and deployment of nuclear weapons and of missiles and aircraft designed primarily to deliver nuclear weapons. This is an essential, verifiable first step lessening the risk of nuclear war and reducing the nuclear arsenals.

from Call to Halt the Nuclear Arms Race

In recent years, various people have been urging the United States to declare a moratorium on the testing, production and deployment of nuclear weapons and weapons systems. In 1979, in the face of a SALT II Treaty that allowed both the US and the Soviet Union to increase their arsenals, a bilateral nuclear weapon freeze appeared to many as an appropriate first step toward disarmament. In December 1979, Sojourners mobilized many people and religious groups to support Senator Mark Hatfield's moratorium amendment to the SALT II Treaty.

A four-page proposal and background paper, "Call to Halt the Nuclear Arms Race,"[1] was prepared in early 1980 by Randall Forsberg of the Institute for Defense and Disarmament Studies. Initially, several prominent persons, including some scientists who had been involved in the Manhattan Project, joined national religious and peace groups in endorsing the call. Several national groups, including FOR, AFSC, and CALC spearheaded national efforts.

Local campaigns of varied sorts began almost immediately. Some people sought individual group endorsements; others printed the call in petition form; some sought public support from local and state governing bodies; and, in western Massachusetts, two local groups began work to place a referendum question on the issue on the November 1980 ballot.

A New Jersey member of the Democratic Party platform committee introduced a plank on the freeze which became the object of a delegate lobbying effort in some states, especially New York and New Jersey. Although it was defeated on the convention floor, the delegates heard passionate speeches by John Kenneth Galbraith, Randall Forsberg, and retired Admiral Gene LaRocque.

Major support for the freeze came from the religious community. A number of prominent religious leaders endorsed it. Five groups — FOR, New Call to Peacemaking, Pax Christi USA, Sojourners, and World Peacemakers — began to investigate ways to further the issue in local congregations. The New Abolitionist Covenant was one result of their joint effort.[2]

At a National Council of Churches Consultation on Disarmament in April 1980, Harvey Cox called for widespread efforts in support of the freeze. In a speech, he said:

> "Enough" has the force of simplicity and logic. It is believable, easy to explain (unlike SALT II) and applies to both sides. Most importantly, it would supply a point of consensus around which Christians of various theologies and traditions could gather. It could unite pacifists, nuclear pacifists and those who believe some military potential is necessary in taking that critical single step *back* from the brink of nuclear war. It is not the Kingdom of God, but it may just avert the Apocalypse.

Subsequently, several national religious groups endorsed the freeze, including the Governing Board of the National Council of Churches and the 1981 General Assemblies of both the United Presbyterian Church in the U.S.A. and the Unitarian Universalist Association.

Only after many local efforts had proceeded and succeeded did any planning for a national strategy begin. In March 1981, over 300 people (many from religious groups) gathered in Washington, D.C., to share experiences and to plan for future nationally-coordinated efforts in support of the freeze.[3] A clearinghouse and coordinating committee have been established.

---

1. Copies available from FOR Disarmament Program (10¢; 10 or more, 8¢ each)

2. See Chapter 6.

3. A copy of the strategy paper and a monthly newsletter are available from the Nuclear Weapon Freeze Clearinghouse.

Further publicity for the freeze was provided by a series of over sixty demonstrations held throughout North America on April 25, 1981. This effort, with the theme "The Future in Our Hands—Freeze the Arms Race", was coordinated by FOR and AFSC, sponsored by the Nuclear Weapons Facilities Task Force. That same weekend hundreds of congregations celebrated Peace Sabbath with programs and services.

People in the religious communities of the US found many ways to further local activities in support of the freeze.

In western Massachusetts, Traprock Peace Center and the regional AFSC initiated a freeze referendum question for the November, 1980, ballot in three state senatorial districts. This question, called Proposition 9, received support from local churches. A special insert for church bulletins was used; religious leaders signed advertisements in local newspapers; the Hampshire Association of the United Church of Christ (representing 28 area Congregational churches) voted its support. These were among the many efforts which resulted in passage of the proposition by a 59% majority.[4]

In Vermont, freeze efforts included some other tactics. David McCauley, field staff for Vermont AFSC, had been using the freeze as a major focus of his peace education work. In February, 1980, the Vermont Ecumenical Council (VEC) Peace Committee hired a full-time staff person for disarmament work in the state's churches. During his year's work he also advocated the freeze as one step toward disarmament.

In summer, 1980, the Vermont AFSC began a petition drive addressed to the state's congressional delegation. Among the first signers were a former governor, the executive minister of the VEC, and the monks of Weston Priory.

To kick off the petition drive, the AFSC and the VEC Peace Committee helped local groups in six towns arrange public meetings from August 6 to 9, 1980. Using the biblical injunction "Choose Life" as a theme, these programs featured the film "War Without Winners" or the slide show "Unforgettable Fire."

Subsequently the AFSC continued aiding individuals and local groups in generating more signatures. The VEC Peace Committee asked regional denominational leaders for their endorsement. As a result, the Executive of the Synod of the Northeast of the United Presbyterian Church wrote to all the state's Presbyterian pastors expressing his support and one United Methodist District Superintendent urged people in his district to support the freeze.

As part of extensive publicity work, the AFSC staff person arranged to be interviewed by the *Vermont Catholic Tribune*. A full page article appeared with a reduced-size petition as a graphic. To everyone's surprise, some people used that graphic to collect signatures. One woman stood outside her church on Sunday and collected signatures on the newspaper.

Meanwhile, other church groups in the state engaged in peace efforts. The Episcopal Commission on World Mission, at the bishop's request, prepared a major recommendation on peace for the May, 1981, diocesan convention. This passed with overwhelming support from the delegates who then proceeded to endorse the freeze without dissent.

The Norwich, VT, Congregational Church was especially involved in the freeze campaign. The pastor had occasionally preached on peace. One member of the congregation, a World War II veteran, had been trying to establish a peace center in town. Together with the church's social action committee, and with the support of the board of deacons, they prepared a resolution on the freeze for the church's annual meeting in January, 1981. At the morning service a week before the meeting, the pastor preached a sermon in support of the freeze; that evening the AFSC staff person led a discussion on the issue. The resolution passed easily and was then referred to the Vermont Conference of the United Church of Christ, which also endorsed the freeze at its April annual meeting.

In Vermont, the town meeting is a venerable tradition, a place for discussion, debate, and voting on local issues, town budgets, and occasionally on state and national issues. In March, 1981, the nuclear weapon freeze issue was raised and passed at 16 town meetings. These efforts were initiated by local people with the assistance of AFSC.

These successes inspired further efforts. Petitions continued to be circulated as people prepared to place the issue before town meetings in 1982. One major event to generate and show support was a 35 mile march from Washington, VT, to Moscow, VT, from August 6 to 9, 1981. An August 7 gathering on the State House lawn in Montpelier brought out thousands to hear the Episcopal bishop, Senator Patrick Leahy, John Kenneth Galbraith, and others. In March, 1982, 159 of the 180 town meetings considering a freeze resolution passed it. In all these efforts, church, peace, and other groups cooperated in generating grassroots concern for disarmament.

On the national level, the United Presbyterian Church in the USA has been prominent in its efforts for peace. In 1980, the church's General Assembly adopted "Peacemaking: The Believers' Calling" as a denominational statement on peace. Subsequent educational efforts at all levels of the church inspired a variety of peace activities. A national Peacemaking Project office, with paid staff, developed materials and provided assistance for local and national church efforts. Many individual Presbyterians were involved in the March, 1981, National Freeze Strategy Conference. At the 1981 General Assembly, at the initiative of several presbyteries, a resolution in support of the freeze was adopted. As a result, copies of the "Call to Halt" were sent to all congregations for their consideration. Many churches, two-thirds of the presbyteries, and all of the church's synods eventually voted their support.[5]

The freeze received an international hearing at the November 23-27, 1981, international hearings on the arms race held by the World Council of Churches in Amsterdam. Randall Forsberg described the freeze as "a dramatic, simple, moderate, but still effective proposal to mobilize the middle class, to give them hope, and to bring them actively into the ranks of those who oppose the arms race." At a November 25 meeting of representatives of the Dutch Interchurch Peace Council (IKV) and of US peace movements, IKV expressed its support of a bilateral freeze and added that a nuclear weapon freeze was also "a step which in our opinion could well be taken independently by either superpower."

---

4. A referendum organizing kit is available from Traprock Peace Center, Keets Road, Deerfield, MA 01342. ($4.50)

5. For additional information, contact The Peacemaking Project, Program Agency UPC-USA, Room 1101, 475 Riverside Drive, New York, NY 10115.

Meanwhile, with a national Freeze Clearinghouse established in St. Louis,[6] a flurry of activities in the US resulted, in mid 1982, in over 2 million signatures on petitions together with the support of numerous town meetings, city and county councils, and with state legislatures. National groups, including the National Council of Black Mayors and the YWCA, and many religious leaders, including over 140 Catholic bishops, had endorsed the freeze.

In 1982, several states were preparing for statewide referendums. In California, efforts for a November referendum generated over 700,000 signatures. As part of this effort, signatures were gathered at Freeze Sabbath sevices held from March 12 to 14.

The freeze also surfaced as a national issue. In March, 1982, Senators Hatfield and Kennedy, with 24 co-sponsors, introduced a freeze resolution in the US Senate; a similar bill in the House of Representatives had 166 co-sponsors. A March 10 press conference revealed the breadth of support, with statements from victims of the atomic bombings, political and scientific leaders, and religious leaders, including Bishop James Armstrong of the National Council of Churches and Rabbi Alexander Schindler of the Union of American Hebrew Congregations. The resolution was subsequently defeated in committee in the Senate. However, it passed in the House Foreign Affairs Committee, only to be defeated by two votes on the House floor in August.

During the United Nations Special Session on Disarmament (UN SSD), in June and July, 1982, there were many public events in support of disarmament. The weekend of May 28-31, before the UN SSD, saw Peace Sabbath celebrations in over 10,000 congregations and many religious witnesses at nuclear weapons facilities. Over 5000 Catholic women religious gathered across from the White House on May 30 as part of a witness "to renew the face of the earth." In New York on June 11, an interfaith religious convocation drew over 10,000 people to a service at the Cathedral of St. John the Divine which was followed by a tree-planting in New York's Central Park. The next day, in what was the largest political gathering in recent US history, over 750,000 gathered in New York urging that the arms race be frozen and reversed. On June 14, several religious contingents were among the 1700 who were arrested while attempting a nonviolent blockade of the UN Missions of the five nuclear powers. And every Friday during the UN SSD, vigils for a freeze were held at the USA and USSR Missions in New York.

At the United Nations itself, Randall Forsberg offered the freeze proposal in her speech during the days set aside for testimony of non-governmental organizations (NGOs). Despite the fact that the UN SSD failed to produce any plan for disarmament, three nations presented freeze proposals which found strong support among many national delegations and NGOs at the UN.

The freeze was an important issue in the 1982 November elections. More than 30% of the electorate had a chance to vote on the freeze. The freeze passed in nine out of the ten states in which it was considered as well as in many other communities, including the District of Columbia. This happened in spite of administration efforts to diffuse the movement with START talks and the "Build now, freeze later" proposals and in spite of efforts to discredit it.

The Nuclear Weapon Freeze Campaign has been the most prominent and newsworthy of recent US disarmament efforts. It has educated and brought together people from diverse backgrounds in efforts to reverse the arms race.[7]

With this momentum, other peace efforts have also grown. Several former policy makers added their public support for demands that the US declare that it will not be the first to use nuclear weapons. Groups in the Nuclear Weapons Facilities Task Force have increased their efforts for the closing and conversion of facilities across the country.[8] People on the Pacific coast have added their voice to the demands for a nuclear-free Pacific from people in Asia, Australia, and Micronesia. Jobs With Peace resolutions have been passed by voters in Boston and throughout the country.[9] There are also efforts for a comprehensive test ban treaty and local campaigns against civil defense planning. And people in the US and European peace movements are planning activities in 1983 to prevent the introduction of Cruise and Pershing II missiles in Europe.

Peacework with the US religious communities has also grown. Many denominations have special peace projects and offices. The National Council of Churches has set aside the week of May 23-29, 1983 as an ecumenical peace week with the theme of "Pursuing Peace with Justice." And the five groups which initiated the New Abolitionist Covenant are reaching out even further into the religious community to promote a faith-based movement against the arms race.

These efforts, building on the widespread support for a nuclear arms freeze, hope to attain a freeze and a reversal of the arms race. The religious communities in the United States have an increasingly vital role in this arduous task of abolishing nuclear weapons.[10]

6. Nuclear Weapon Freeze Clearinghouse, 4144 Lindell Blvd., St. Louis, MO 63108

7. Contact FOR's Disarmament Program for buttons (50¢), posters (25¢), and other resources.
8. Nuclear Weapons Facilities Task Force, FOR, Box 271, Nyack, NY 10960.
9. Jobs With Peace Campaign, 77 Summer St., Boston, MA 02110.
10. See also senators Mark Hatfield and Edward Kennedy, *Freeze: How You Can Help Prevent Nuclear War.* (Bantam. $3.50)

6. The New Abolitionist Covenant

In November 1980, representatives of five religious peace groups — Fellowship of Reconciliation, New Call to Peacemaking, Pax Christi USA, Sojourners, and World Peacemakers — began meeting to consider how they might stimulate peace work in U.S. churches, synagogues, and meetings, especially at the local level. They all shared a commitment to peacemaking and saw a nuclear weapon freeze as a viable first step toward disarmament, but they wanted to find ways to reach out to local congregations.

Among their first activities was the promotion of the U.S. version of the World Peace Pledge: "In light of my faith, I am prepared to live without nuclear weapons in my country." Plans were made to collect signatures to this pledge that would be presented to officials at the United Nations and the White House at the time of the U.N. Second Special Session on Disarmament in May 1982.

After meeting for several months, the representatives of these five groups decided to enter into a "covenant" which would express both the spiritual bases of their peace work and their commitment to act toward the abolition of nuclear weapons.

The covenant document was further refined so that it could be presented to others to challenge them to acknowledge that the abolition of nuclear weapons is an urgent matter of faith. In August 1981, the five groups began distributing this New Abolitionist Covenant.

The Covenant began as a specifically Christian document, expressing the faith of those involved in the original meetings. The Fellowship of Reconciliation prepared an interfaith version so that people from a variety of religious traditions could be approached with the Covenant. Both versions of the Covenant follow.

Since the Covenant grew out of a series of prayerful meetings, those who wrote it hope that others will follow a similar process as they consider the New Abolitionist Covenant.

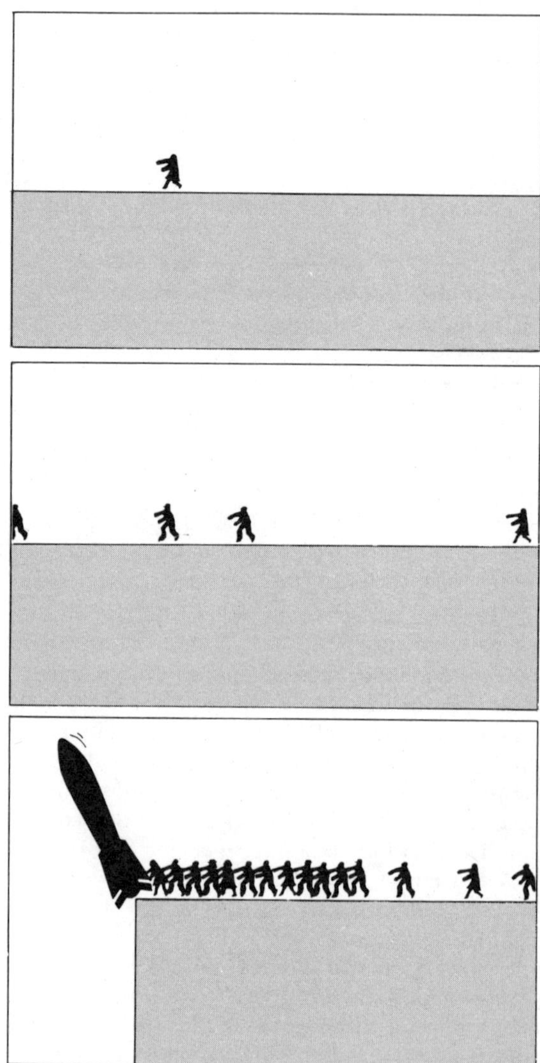

First, take some time and read the Covenant prayerfully. Then share it with friends, perhaps as part of an evening of prayer or recollection. Give a copy to your rabbi or pastor or to your parish council or congregational board. Seek to involve them in a prayerful discussion of the Covenant.

Afterwards, find some people who wish to enter into a covenantal relationship, using the New Abolitionist Covenant as the basis. This group might meet several times to pray over the Covenant and to find ways to implement the six commitments contained in it. (Refer to chapters two to four of this handbook for specific ideas.)

The five groups involved in formulating this Covenant will be continuing their meetings to find ways to further the commitment of the religious communities of this country to disarmament. Contact any of them for further information in this effort.

Texts of the New Abolitionist Covenant

In the name of God, let us abolish nuclear weapons.

Interfaith Version

Faith must be demonstrated anew in each historical moment. Our faith must always be addressed to the time in which we live. We must always find ways to relate timeless but timely faith to our own situation, showing what we will embrace and what we will refuse.

Some historical issues stand out as particularly urgent among the fundamental concerns of people of faith. These overarching moral questions intrude upon the routine of life and plead for the compassion and courage of God's people everywhere. The nuclear arms race is such a question today.

In the 19th century, thousands of people from diverse religious traditions came to believe that slavery was an evil that challenged the very integrity of their faith. They believed that for any person to claim ownership of another human being denied the belief that each person is loved by God and made in God's image. They began to preach that to be faithful meant to turn away from the institution of slavery, to refuse to cooperate with it, and to work for its abolition. Though this seemed like an absurd, unattainable goal, these people insisted that God required nothing less. They came to be called abolitionists.

Today, acceptance of nuclear weapons has brought us also to a crisis of faith. The nuclear threat is not just a political issue any more than slavery was. It is a question that challenges everything we say about our belief in God. In other words, the growing prospect of nuclear war presents us with more than a test of survival; it confronts us with a test of our faith.

Nuclear war is total war. Unlimited in their violence, indiscriminate in their victims, uncontrollable in their devastation, nuclear weapons have brought humanity to a historical crossroads. More than at any previous time in history, the alternatives are peace and destruction. In a nuclear war, there are no winners.

We are people of faith who now see that the nuclear arms race is more than a question of public policy. We believe the wholesale destruction threatened by these weapons makes their possession and planned use morally indefensible and an offense against God and humanity. Through deliberation and prayer, we have become convinced that the call to be peacemakers urgently needs to be renewed in the temples, churches, and meetings of this country and made specific by a commitment to abolish nuclear weapons and to find a new basis for national security.

As the foundation of national security, nuclear weapons are idolatrous. As a method of defense, they are

Christian Version

The Christian faith must be demonstrated anew in each historical moment. The gospel is always addresssed to the time in which we live. Christians must find ways to relate timeless but timely faith to their own situation, showing what they will embrace and what they will refuse because of Jesus Christ.

Some historical issues stand out as particularly urgent among the church's fundamental concerns. These overarching moral questions intrude upon the routine of the church's life and plead for the compassion and courage of God's people everywhere. Slavery was such a question for Christians in the 19th century. The nuclear arms race is such a question today.

Thousands of Christians from diverse traditions came to see that slavery was an evil that challenged the very integrity of their faith. They believed that for any person to claim ownership of another human being denied that each person is beloved by God and made in God's image. These Christians began to preach that to follow Christ meant to turn away from the institution of slavery, to refuse to cooperate with it, and to work for its abolition. Though this seemed like an absurd, unattainable goal, they insisted that God required nothing less. They came to be called abolitionists.

Christian acceptance of nuclear weapons has brought us also to a crisis of faith. The nuclear threat is not just a political issue any more than slavery was. It is a question that challenges our worship of God and our commitment to Jesus Christ. In other words, the growing prospect of nuclear war presents us with more than a test of survival; it confronts us with a test of faith.

Nuclear war is total war. Unlimited in their violence, indiscriminate in their victims, uncontrollable in their devastation, nuclear weapons have brought humanity to a historical crossroads. More than at any previous time in history, the alternatives are peace or destruction. In nuclear war there are no winners.

We are Christians who now see that the nuclear arms race is more than a question of public policy. We believe that the wholesale destruction threatened by these weapons makes their possession and planned use an offense against God and humanity, no matter what the provocation or political justification. Through deliberation and prayer we have become convinced that Jesus' call to be peacemakers urgently needs to be renewed in the churches and made specific by a commitment to abolish nuclear weapons and to find a new basis of national security.

suicidal. The threatened nuclear annihilation of whole populations in the name of national security is an evil we can no longer accept. At stake is whether we trust in God or the bomb. We can no longer profess our faith and depend on nuclear weapons to save us. Conversion in our day must include turning away from nuclear weapons as we turn to God.

The building and threatened use of nuclear weapons is a sin — against God, against God's creatures, and God's creation. There is no theology or doctrine in any religious tradition that could ever justify nuclear war. Whether one begins with pacifism or with the just war doctrine, total destruction by nuclear weapons is morally unacceptable.

We fail to realize that the bomb has already deeply affected us. For in accepting its presence and proliferation, we have accepted the spiritual death it brings and entered a condition that the Bible calls "hardness of heart." We can live with the presence of nuclear weapons among us and be prepared to use them again only if we are willing to allow our human compassion and our basic moral values to die.

The God of the Bible loves the poor and demands justice for them. To continue to spend hundreds of billions of dollars preparing for war while millions go hungry is a grievous failure of compassion and an affront to God. But with God's grace, our hearts can be softened in order to heed the biblical vision of converting the weapons of war into instruments of peace.

To believe that nuclear weapons can solve international problems is the height of unreality and naivete. When nuclear war is thinkable, folly and madness have become the accepted political wisdom. It is time for people of faith to bear witness to the vision of God's peace which can provide hope for us in breaking the hold of the political realities in whose name we march to oblivion.

In times past, people from many religious traditions have joined together to oppose great social evils and to point the way to change. We believe the growing prospect of nuclear war now calls for such unity of religious response in showing another way.

Our response as people of faith begins with repentance for almost four decades of accepting nuclear weapons. Repentance in a nuclear age means non-cooperation with preparations for nuclear war and the turning of our lives toward peace.

Whatever we say to the government must be based first on what we ourselves have publicly committed ourselves to do and not to do in the face of a nuclear war. The fruits of our repentance will be made visible in our active witness and leadership for peace.

No longer trusting in nuclear weapons, we refuse to cooperate with preparations for total war. Trusting anew in God, we begin cooperating with one another in preparations for peace. We covenant together to work for peace. We join with one another to make these vital commitments.

As the foundation of national security, nuclear weapons are idolatrous. As a method of defense, they are suicidal. To believe that nuclear weapons can solve international problems is the greatest illusion and the height of naivete.

The threatened nuclear annihilation of whole populations in the name of national security is an evil we can no longer accept. At stake is whether we trust in God or the bomb. We can no longer confess Jesus as Lord and depend on nuclear weapons to save us. Conversion in our day must include turning away from nuclear weapons as we turn to Jesus Christ.

The building and threatened use of nuclear weapons is a sin against God, God's creatures, and God's creation. There is no theology or doctrine in the traditions of the church that could ever justify nuclear war. Whether one begins with pacifism or with the just war doctrine, nuclear weapons are morally unacceptable.

The God of the Bible loves the poor and demands justice for the oppressed. To continue to spend hundreds of billions of dollars in preparation for war while millions go hungry is a grievous failure of compassion and an affront to God. But by God's grace our hearts can be softened in order to heed the biblical vision of converting the weapons of war into instruments of peace.

When nuclear war is thinkable, folly and madness have become the accepted political wisdom. It is time for the church to bear witness to the absolute character of the word of God which is finally our only hope in breaking the hold of the political realities in whose name we march to oblivion.

In times past, Christians from many traditions joined together to oppose great social sin and point the way to change. We believe the growing prospect of nuclear war now calls for such unity of Christian response.

Our response as Christians begins with repentance for almost four decades of accepting nuclear weapons. Repentance in a nuclear age means non-cooperation with preparations for nuclear war and the turning of our lives toward peace.

Whatever we say to the government must be based first on what we have publicly committed ourselves to do and not to do in the face of a nuclear war. The fruits of our repentance will be made visible in our active witness and leadership for peace.

No longer trusting in nuclear weapons, we refuse to cooperate with preparations for total war. Trusting anew in God, we will begin cooperating with one another in preparations for peace. We covenant to work together for peace and join with one another to make these vital commitments.

1. Prayer

We covenant together to pray. Prayer is at the heart of religious peacemaking. Prayer can change us and our relationships. Prayer begins in confession for our sins and extends into intercession for our enemies, bringing them closer to us. We will pray, asking God to hold back the nuclear devastation so that we may turn from our folly. Through prayer, the reality of the power of faith can be established in our lives and free us to participate in the work of reconciliation in the world.

2. Education

We covenant together to learn. Our ignorance and passivity must be transformed into awareness and responsibility. We must act together to dispel our blindness and hardness of heart. We will ground ourselves in the biblical, theological, and moral bases for peacemaking. We will become thoroughly and deeply informed about the dangers of the arms race and the steps to be taken toward peace. We will become aware of the teaching of our religious traditions on the matter of nuclear warfare.

3. Spiritual examination

We covenant together to examine ourselves. To shed the light of faith on the nuclear situation, we will examine the basic decisions of our personal lives in regard to our jobs, our lifestyles, our taxes, and our relationships to see where and how we are cooperating with preparations for nuclear war. Concerned with the spiritual wellbeing of our brothers and sisters whose lives and livelihood are now dependent upon the nuclear war system, we will undertake a thorough pastoral evaluation of the life of our congregations in all these matters.

4. Testimony

We covenant together to spread the good news of peace. We will speak out and reach out to our friends, our families, our sisters and brothers in faith about the dangers of the nuclear arms buildup and the urgency of peace. We will take the message to other worship communities in our neighborhoods, to our denominations, and to their decision-making bodies on every level. The causes of peace will be preached from our pulpits, lifted up in our prayers, and made part of our worship. We will offer faith in God as an alternative to trust in the bomb.

5. Public Witness

We covenant together to bear public witness. Our opposition to nuclear weapons and the imperative of peace will be taken into the public arena: to our work places, to our community and civic organizations, to the

1. Prayer

We covenant together to pray. Prayer is at the heart of Christian peacemaking. Prayer can change us and our relationships. Prayer begins in confession of our own sin and extends into intercession for our enemies, bringing them closer to us. We will pray, asking God to hold back the nuclear devastation so that we may turn from our folly. Through prayer, the reality of Christ's victory over nuclear darkness can be established in our lives and free us to participate in Christ's reconciling work in the world.

2. Education

We covenant together to learn. Our ignorance and passivity must be transformed into awareness and responsibility. We must act together to dispel our blindness and hardness of heart. We will ground ourselves in the biblical and theological basis for peacemaking. We will become thoroughly and deeply informed about the danger of the arms race and the steps to be taken toward peace. We will become aware of the churches' teachings on the matter of nuclear warfare.

3. Spiritual examination

We covenant together to examine ourselves. To shed the light of the gospel on the nuclear situation, we will examine the basic decisions of our personal lives in regard to our jobs, lifestyles, taxes, and relationships, to see where and how we are cooperating with preparations for nuclear war. The church should be concerned with the spiritual wellbeing of its members whose livelihoods are now dependent on the nuclear war system. We will undertake a thorough pastoral evaluation of the life of our congregations in all these matters.

4. Evangelism

We covenant together to spread the gospel of peace. We will speak out and reach out to our friends, families, and Christian brothers and sisters about the dangers of the nuclear arms buildup and the urgency of peace. We will take the message to the other churches in our neighborhoods, to our denominations, and to the decision-making bodies of our churches on every level. The cause of peace will be preached from our pulpits, lifted up in our prayers, and made part of our worship. We will offer faith in God as an alternative to trust in the bomb.

5. Public witness

We covenant together to bear public witness. Our opposition to nuclear weapons and the imperative of peace will be taken into the public arena: to our work places, to our community and civic organizations, to the media, to our governmental bodies, to the streets, and to

media, to our governmental bodies, to the streets, and to the nuclear facilities themselves. A prayerful presence for peace needs to be established at all those places where nuclear weapons are researched, produced, stored, and deployed, and where decisions are made to continue the arms race. The gatherings, events, and institutions of our religious bodies will also become important places for our public witness. We will make our convictions known at all these places, especially on significant dates in the religious calendar and on August 6 and 9, the anniversaries of the bombings of Hiroshima and Nagasaki.

6. Nuclear disarmament

We covenant together to work to stop the arms race. In light of our faith, we are prepared to live without nuclear weapons. We will publicly advocate a nuclear weapon freeze as the first step toward abolishing nuclear weapons altogether. We will act in our local communities to place the call for a nuclear weapon freeze on the public agenda. We will press our government and the other nuclear powers to halt all further testing, production, and deployment of nuclear weapons and then move steadily and rapidly to eliminate them completely.

We recognize a call from God to make these commitments and with the help of God we hope to fulfill them. Rooted in our faith in God and strengthened by the hope that comes from our faith, we covenant together to make peace.

the nuclear weapons facilities themselves. A prayerful presence for peace needs to be established at all those places where nuclear weapons are researched, produced, stored, and deployed, and where decisions are made to continue the arms race.

The gatherings, events, and institutions of the churches will also become important places for our public witness. We will make our convictions known at all these places, especially on significant dates in the church calendar and on August 6 and 9, the anniversaries of the bombings of Hiroshima and Nagasaki.

6. Nuclear disarmament

We covenant together to work to stop the arms race. In light of our faith, we are prepared to live without nuclear weapons. We will publicly advocate a nuclear weapons freeze as the first step toward abolishing nuclear weapons altogether. We will act in our local communities to place the call for a nuclear weapons freeze on the public agenda. We will press our government and the other nuclear powers to halt all further testing, production, and deployment of nuclear weapons, and then move steadily and rapidly to eliminate them completely.

We recognize a call from God to make these simple commitments and, through the grace of God, we hope to fulfill them. Rooted in the gospel of Jesus Christ and strengthened by the hope that comes from faith, we covenant together to make peace.

Copies of the New Abolitionist Covenant are available from the FOR's Covenant Peacemaking Program for 30¢ each; 10 to 99 copies are 20¢ each; and 100 or more copies are 10¢ each. Postage is included in these prices. Please indicate whether you want the Interfaith or specifically Christian version.

A Resource Guide for the New Abolitionist Covenant is available from FOR in both an Interfaith and a specifically Christian version. Prices are the same as those for copies of the Covenant. Please indicate which version you wish when ordering.

Selected Resources

Books

Robert Aldridge, *Counterforce Syndrome: A Guide to U.S. Nuclear Weapons and Strategic Doctrine.* (Institute for Policy Studies. $4.95) *

Richard Barnet. *Real Security; Restoring American Power in a Dangerous Decade.* (Touchstone. $4.95)

Helen Caldicott, *Nuclear Madness: What You Can Do!* (Bantam. $2.95) *

John Donaghy, ed., *To Proclaim Peace; Religious Statements on the Arms Race.* (Revised edition) (Fellowship of Reconciliation. $2)*

John Ferguson, *The Politics of Love: The New Testament and Nonviolent Revolution.* (Fellowship. $3) * *War and Peace in the World's Religions.* (Oxford. $3.95) *

W. H. Ferry, *Farewell to Arms: A Case for Unilateral Disarmament.* (Fellowship. $1) *

Robert Heyer, ed., *Nuclear Disarmament: Key Statements of Popes, Bishops, Councils, and Churches.* (Paulist. $7.95)

Robert Johansen. *Toward a Dependable Peace: A Proposal for an Appropriate Security System.* (Institute for World Order. $1.50) *

Thomas Merton, *Faith and Violence: Christian Teaching and Christian Practice.* (University of Notre Dame Press. $3.45) *

The Nonviolent Alternative. (Farrar, Straus & Giroux, paper. $7.95)

Thomas Merton, ed., *Gandhi on Nonviolence.* (New Directions. $2.95)

Jane Rockman, ed., *Peace in Search of Makers: Riverside Church Reverse the Arms Race Convocation.* (Judson Press. $5.95)

Jonathan Schell, *The Fate of the Earth.* (Avon. $2.95)

Arthur Simon, *Bread for the World.* (Paulist Press. $2.95)

Ruth Leger Sivard, *World Military and Social Expenditures* (annual). (WMSE publications. $4) *

Allan Solomonow, ed., *Roots of Jewish Nonviolence.* (Jewish Peace Fellowship. $2) *

E. P. Thompson & Dan Smith, ed., *Protest and Survive.* (Monthly Review Press. $4.95) *

Jim Wallis, ed., *Waging Peace: A Handbook for the Struggle Against Nuclear Weapons.* (Harper & Row. $4.95)

Makers of the Nuclear Holocaust: A Guide to the Nuclear Weapons Complex and Citizen Action. (Fellowship of Reconciliation. $1.25) *

Peacemaking: The Believers' Calling. (Office of the General Assembly, United Presbyterian Church in the U.S.A., 475 Riverside Drive, New York, NY 10115. $1.25)

To Proclaim Peace: Religious Statements on Disarmament. (FOR, $1; 10 or more, 75¢ each) *

Unforgettable Fire: Pictures Drawn by Atomic Bomb Survivors. (Pantheon. $7.95)

Words of Conscience: Religious Statements on Conscientious Objection. (NISBCO $2)*

---

*Available from FOR: please add 20% for postage and handling.

Periodicals

Fellowship, Box 271, Nyack, NY 10960 ($10/year)

The Catholic Worker, 36 E. First St., New York, NY 10003 (25¢/yr)

The Defense Monitor, Center for Defense Information, 122 Maryland Ave. NE, Washington, DC 20002

Friends Journal, 152-A North 15th St., Philadelphia, PA 19102 ($12/yr)

IFOR Report, International Fellowship of Reconciliation, Hof Van Sonoy, 1811-LD Alkmaar, The Netherlands. ($15/yr)

Menorah: Sparks of Jewish Renewal, Public Resource Center, 1747 Connecticut Avenue NW, Washington, DC 20009. ($24/yr)

The Progressive, 409 East Main Street, Madison, WI 53703. ($20/yr)

Sojourners, P.O. Box 29272, Washington, DC 20017 ($12/year)

Articles on peace-related issues appear in many other publications, including *Christianity & Crisis, Israel Horizons, The Other Side, Genesis 2, Bulletin of the Atomic Scientists, In These Times, The Nation,* and *WIN.*

Audiovisual Resources

Every Heart Beats True: Christian Perspectives on Military Service. (Slide show on draft issues from a Christian perspective for high school students). FOR: $12 rental; Packard Manse: $53 sale; $15 rental)

Excuse Me, America! (46-minute film featuring Dom Helder Camara speaking on his nonviolent commitment and the poor.) (FOR: $50 rental negotiable)

The Last Epidemic. (Film or video-tape, based on a Physicians for Social Responsibility conference in San Francisco.) (Resource Center for Nonviolence, Box 2324, Santa Cruz, CA 95063 and many peace groups.)

The Last Slide Show. (20-minute slide show on nuclear power and weapons; up-beat.) (FOR: $12 rental; Packard Manse: $53 sale, $15 rental.)

Shalom (filmstrip and record on the biblical vision on peace) (FOR: $12 rental)

Paul Jacobs and the Nuclear Gang. (60-minute film on the hazards of radiation, narrated by a journalist who himself became a victim.) (FOR: rental for 50% of proceeds plus shipping)

War Without Winners. (28-minute film on the nuclear arms race narrated by retired Admiral Gene LaRocque.) (Center for Defense Information and many local AFSC offices; rental varies)

Hiroshima-Nagasaki, 1945. (Graphic film on the effects of the use of the first atomic weapons.) (Wilmington College Peace Center: $15 rental)

Unforgettable Fire: Drawings of Hiroshima. (Moving slides drawn by survivors of the Hiroshima bombing, with narration.) (CALC: $7.00 rental)

For more information:
John Dowling, *War/Peace Film Guide.* (World Without War Publications. $5.00) *
Packard Manse Media Project, Box 450, Stoughton, MA 02072.
Wilmington College Peace Resource Center, Pyle Center Box 1183, Wilmington, OH 45177.

FOR Brochures

Available from FOR 10¢ each; 100 or more, 5¢ each.
Economic Conversion: Turning from War to Peace.
Reversing the Arms Race: The Case for Disarmament Initiatives.
Proclaiming Shalom: A Speakers Bureau for the Religious Community.
World Peace Pledge brochure.
FOR/AFSC Nuclear Weapons Facilities Project.
FOR Statements on Registration and the Draft.
Instead of the Death Penalty.
The Middle East Arms Connection. (25¢; 5/$1; 25/$3)

Organizations

1. The Fellowship of Reconciliation,
   Box 271, Nyack, NY 10960.
   The FOR has local and regional offices in over 65 cities around the country. Contact the FOR for names and addresses of people in your area.

   International Fellowship of Reconciliation,
   Hof Van Sonoy, 1811-LD, Alkmaar, The Netherlands

2. *New Abolitionist Covenant Groups:*
   Fellowship of Reconciliation, Box 271, Nyack, NY 10960
   New Call to Peacemaking, Box 1245, Elkhart, IN 46518
   Pax Christi USA, 6337 W. Cornelia, Chicago, IL 60634
   Sojourners, P.O. Box 29272, Washington, DC 20017
   World Peacemakers, 2025 Massachusetts Ave., N.W., Washington, D.C. 20036

3. *Other groups working in the religious community:*
   American Friends Service Committee, 1501 Cherry St., Philadelphia, PA 19102
   Clergy and Laity Concerned, 198 Broadway, New York, NY 10038
   Interfaith Center to Reverse the Arms Race, 132 N. Euclid Ave., Pasadena, CA 91101
   Mennonite Central Committee, (US) Peace Section, 21 South 12th St., Akron, PA 17501

New Jewish Agenda, 1123 Broadway, Suite 1217, New York, NY 10010
Riverside Church Disarmament Program, 490 Riverside Drive, New York, NY 10027
Religious Task Force, 85 S. Oxford St., Brooklyn, NY 11217
World Conference on Religion and Peace, 777 UN Plaza, New York, NY 10017

4. *Other groups (see also addresses listed in Chapters 3 and 4):*
   Center for Defense Information, 303 Capital Gallery, 600 Maryland Avenue SW, Washington, DC 20024
   Coalition for a New Foreign and Military Policy, 120 Maryland Avenue NE, Washington, DC 20002
   Council on Economic Priorities, 84 Fifth Avenue, New York, NY 10011
   Institute for Defense and Disarmament Studies, 251 Harvard Street, Brookline, MA 02146
   Institute for World Order, 777 UN Plaza, New York, NY 10017
   Jonah House, 1933 Park Avenue, Baltimore, MD 21217
   Martin Luther King, Jr. Center for Nonviolent Social Change, 449 Auburn Ave., N.E., Atlanta, GA 30312
   Middle East Peace Project, 339 Lafayette Street, New York, NY 10012
   Mobilization for Survival, 853 Broadway, Suite 2109, New York, NY 10003
   NARMIC/AFSC, 1501 Cherry Street, Philadelphia, PA 19102
   Nuclear Weapon Freeze Clearinghouse, 4144 Lindell Blvd., St. Louis, MO 63108
   Physicians for Social Responsibility, 693 Massachusetts Avenue, Cambridge, MA 02139
   Project Ploughshares, Institute for Peace and Conflict Studies, Conrad Grebel College, Waterloo, Ontario N2L, 3GC, Canada
   SANE, 514 C Street NE, Washington, DC 20002
   Southern Christian Leadership Conference, 333 Auburn Ave., N.E., Atlanta, GA 30303
   Union of Concerned Scientists, 1384 Massachusetts Avenue, Cambridge 02238
   United Nations Association USA, 300 E. 42nd Street, New York, NY 10017
   War Resisters League, 339 Lafayette Street, New York, NY 10012
   Women's International League for Peace and Freedom, 1213 Race Street, Philadelphia, PA 19107

5. *Religious Peace Fellowships*
   Baptist Peace Fellowship, 115 N. Broadway, Nyack NY 10960
   Brethren Peace Fellowship, Box 415, New Windsor, MD 21776
   Buddhist Peace Fellowship, Box 4650, Berkeley, CA 94704
   Catholic Peace Fellowship, 339 Lafayette St., New York, NY 10012
   Church of God Peace Fellowship, 1303 E. 5th St., Anderson, IN 46011

Disciples Peace Fellowship, Box 1986, Indianapolis, IN 46206

Episcopal Peace Fellowship, Wisconsin Ave. & Woodley Rd. NW, Washington, DC 20016

Jewish Peace Fellowship, Box 271, Nyack, NY 10960

Lutheran Peace Fellowship, 168 West 100th St., New York, NY 10025

Southern Presbyterian Peace Fellowship, 1808 Stokes Lane, Nashville, TN 37215

Unitarian-Universalist Peace Fellowship, 12861 Titian, Granada Hills, CA 91344

United Methodist Peace Fellowship, 5123 Truman Rd., Kansas City, MO 64127

United Presbyterian Peace Fellowship, Box 271, Nyack, NY 10960

Other peace fellowships are in formation, including a Reformed Peace Fellowship, a United Church of Christ Peace Fellowship, and a Jain Peace Fellowship. For information on any of these, contact: Director of Interfaith Activities, Fellowship of Reconciliation, Box 271, Nyack, NY 10960.

THE FELLOWSHIP OF RECONCILIATION is composed of men and women who recognize the essential unity of all humanity and have joined together to explore the power of love and truth for resolving human conflict. While it has always been vigorous in its opposition to war, the Fellowship has insisted equally that this effort must be based on a commitment to the achieving of a peaceful world community, with full dignity and freedom for every human being.

The FELLOWSHIP OF RECONCILIATION was founded in Cambridge, England in 1914 when Henry Hodgkin, an English Quaker, and Friedrich Sigmund-Schultze, a German Lutheran pastor, pledged to remain friends and continue to work for peace, even though their countries were at war. The following year the FOR was established in the United States. FOR groups have subsequently been organized in 27 countries, with an international secretariat in Holland.

IF YOU AGREE with the principles of the Fellowship of Reconciliation, we invite you to become a member by signing a membership card. There are no required annual dues. However, the FOR is a working Fellowship, dependent for financial support on the contributions of its members and friends. Please write for further information, a membership application, a listing of the more than 50 local FOR chapters, and a sample copy of **Fellowship** magazine.

From the FELLOWSHIP OF RECONCILIATION Statement of Purpose   **Box 271, Nyack, NY 10960**   **(914) 358-4601**

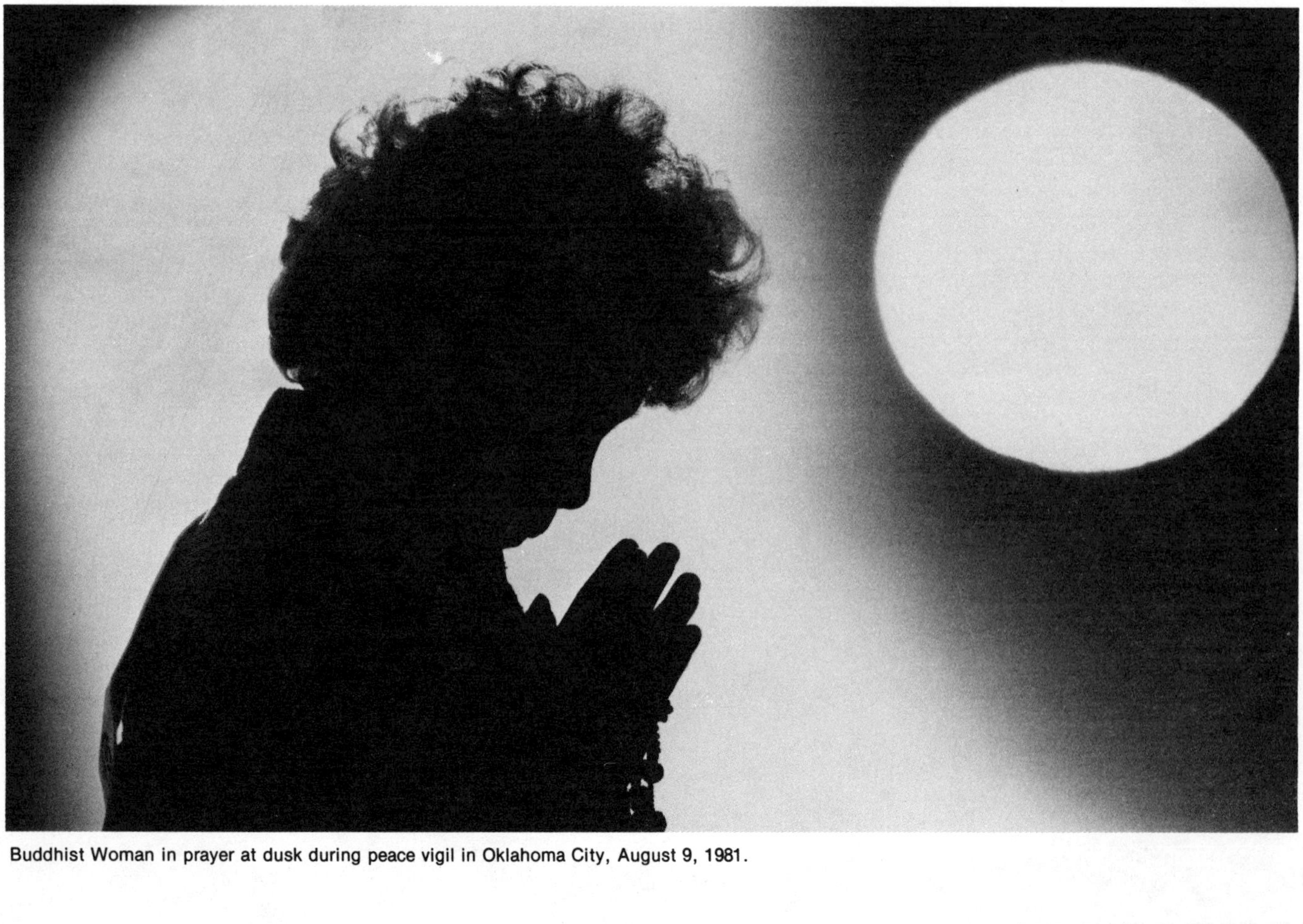

Buddhist Woman in prayer at dusk during peace vigil in Oklahoma City, August 9, 1981.